FIRMINO

MATT AND TOM OLDFIELD

ULTIMATE
FOOTBALL HEROES

FIRMINO

FROM THE PLAYGROUND
TO THE PITCH

DINO

First published in the UK in 2020 by Dino Books,
an imprint of Bonnier Books UK
The Plaza, 535 King's Road, London SW10 0SZ
Owned by Bonnier Books
Sveavägen 56, Stockholm, Sweden

@dinobooks
@footieheroesbks
heroesfootball.com
www.bonnierbooks.co.uk

Design by www.envydesign.co.uk

Paperback ISBN: 978 1 78946 232 6
E-book ISBN: 978 1 78946 233 3

British Library Cataloguing-in-Publication Data:
A catalogue record for this book is available from the British Library.

Printed and bound in Great Britain by Clays Ltd, Elcograf S.p.A.

1 3 5 7 9 10 8 6 4 2

MIX
Paper from
responsible sources
FSC® C018072
www.fsc.org

For all readers, young and old(er)

Matt Oldfield delivers sports writing workshops in schools, and is the author of *Unbelievable Football* and *Johnny Ball: Accidental Football Genius*. Tom Oldfield is a freelance sports writer and the author of biographies on Cristiano Ronaldo, Arsène Wenger and Rafael Nadal.

Cover illustration by Dan Leydon
To learn more about Dan visit danleydon.com
To purchase his artwork visit etsy.com/shop/footynews

TABLE OF CONTENTS

ACKNOWLEDGEMENTS

First of all, I'd like to thank Bonnier Books UK for supporting me throughout and for running the ever-expanding UFH ship so smoothly. Writing stories for the next generation of football fans is both an honour and a pleasure.

I wouldn't be doing this if it wasn't for my brother Tom. I owe him so much and I'm very grateful for his belief in me as an author. I feel like Robin setting out on a solo career after a great partnership with Batman. I hope I do him (Tom, not Batman) justice with these new books.

Next up, I want to thank my friends for keeping me sane during long hours in front of the laptop.

Pang, Will, Mills, Doug, John, Charlie – the laughs and the cups of coffee are always appreciated.

I've already thanked my brother but I'm also very grateful to the rest of my family, especially Melissa, Noah and of course Mum and Dad. To my parents, I owe my biggest passions: football and books. They're a real inspiration for everything I do.

Finally, I couldn't have done this without Iona's encouragement and understanding during long, work-filled weekends. Much love to you.

CHAPTER 1

CLUB CHAMPIONS OF THE WORLD!

Club Champions of the World!

A loud cheer went up around the packed stadium as Jordan Henderson led the Liverpool team out on to the pitch for the 2019 FIFA Club World Cup Final. The 45,000 spectators couldn't wait to watch the European Champions in action.

Manager Jürgen Klopp had picked a strong team for the big match, full of entertaining superstars: the amazing goalkeeper, Alisson; the classy centre-back, Virgil van Dijk; and flying full-backs, Trent Alexander-Arnold and Andy Robertson. Most famous of all were the fab front three: Sadio Mané, Mo Salah and Roberto Firmino. When they played together, Liverpool always scored, and they almost always won.

Although Sadio and Mo usually got more of the goals and the glory, everyone knew that Roberto Firmino was an equally important player. He connected with his teammates like the conductor in an orchestra. Without him, Liverpool simply weren't the same team. Firmino had the speed and skill to lead the counter-attacks, and the grit and determination to form the first line of their defence. Liverpool was very lucky to have him; there was no-one else quite like him in the world!

And Roberto had three major reasons to feel extra excited about the Club World Cup Final:

1) He had the chance to win a fourth top trophy of the year,

2) He had already scored the winner in the semi-final against Monterrey,

and 3) Liverpool were taking on the South American champions, Flamengo, who were from Brazil, just like him!

Roberto was lining up against several of his national

teammates: Gabriel Barbosa, Filipe Luís, Diego Alves, Rafinha… it was like a *Seleção* reunion! Although it was nice to see so many familiar faces, it also made him even more determined to win. After all, if Liverpool lost, he would never hear the end of it!

Plus, Roberto wanted to put on a show for all the people watching back in Brazil. He had recently helped his country to win the 2019 Copa América, but he hadn't played club football in his homeland since the age of eighteen. After his first senior season at Figueirense, he had joined German club Hoffenheim to try and make it big in Europe. And look at him now – he was a Champions League winner!

Back in Brazil, however, he still wasn't at that superstar level with Neymar Jr and his friend Philippe Coutinho. Not yet, anyway.

'This is my time to shine!' Firmino thought as he raced forward, right from the kick-off.

And his first scoring chance arrived straight away. Joe Gomez's long ball from the back flew all the way over the Flamengo defence and dropped down in front of Roberto inside the penalty area. Wow, what an opportunity to give Liverpool the lead! He chested the ball down beautifully, but when he saw the keeper rushing out towards him, he lost his cool and skied his shot high over the crossbar.

'Nooooo!' he groaned as he skidded across the grass on his knees.

It was a massive opportunity wasted, and Roberto regretted it more and more as the first half went on. Hopefully, he could make up for it in the second...

He ran into the Flamengo box, flicked the ball brilliantly over the defender's head and then fired off a left-foot shot. The keeper could only stand and watch as the ball flew straight past him... but bounced back off the post and then off the pitch for a goal kick.

What?! Roberto couldn't believe it, but he didn't stop for a strop. Instead, he kept going, hunting for his next chance.

At last, it arrived, in the first half of extra time. As Hendo played a long pass towards Sadio, Roberto was only just crossing the halfway line. But by the time Sadio controlled it and looked up for support, Roberto had sprinted forwards to the edge of the box to help him.

'Yes!'

Again, Roberto was one-on-one with the Flamengo keeper. This time, he didn't panic and blast the ball high and wide. Instead, he fooled everyone by calmly cutting inside. Then, with the keeper stranded on the floor, he fired a shot into the empty net to break millions of Brazilian hearts.

Goooooooooooooooooooaaaaaaaaaaaaaaaalllllllllllll llllllllllllll!!!!!!!!!!!!!!!!!!!

Once he had seen the ball safely cross the line, Roberto ripped off his shirt and leapt high into the air, his trademark smile replaced by a look of pure passion. Yes, he had done it – he had made up for his earlier miss, and now Liverpool were minutes away from becoming the Club Champions of the World!

At the final whistle, there were hugs and high-fives all around. Job done – would Roberto ever get tired of that trophy-winning feeling? No, never! The biggest moments of the biggest games – that's when he was at his best. The boy from Maceió was a born matchwinner.

CHAPTER 2

MAMÃE'S BOY IN MACEIÓ

'Roberto! Roberto!' Mariana called out from the doorstep of the Firmino family home.

School had long since finished for the day and her son was supposed to be home by now. So, where was he? Roberto was nearly nine years old and tended to rush around eagerly like a happy, hungry rabbit, making it hard for Mariana to keep a close eye on him and make sure that he stayed safe.

As she kept telling Roberto, there were two sides to the city of Maceió. On the one side, you had the sun, the clear, turquoise sea, and the beautiful, sandy beaches. That's why they called their area 'Brazil's Caribbean'. But on the other side, not far from the fancy waterfront bars and hotels, was the neighbourhood of Trapiche da Barra, where families like the Firminos lived in poverty. Their homes were crumbling and cramped, and their streets were lined with litter and dirty water. Often, the local people didn't have enough money to pay for electricity or food.

For young boys like Roberto, Maceió could be a very dangerous city to grow up in. There was violence all around and if kids weren't careful, they could get caught up in the world of crime. For Mariana Firmino, keeping Roberto away from the local gangs was a priority. And if he was ever late getting home, she soon started to worry...

'I'm here, Mamãe!' Roberto shouted out suddenly as he raced around the corner and into Mariana's arms.

'Good boy,' she said, giving him a big hug. 'But next time, you come straight home from school, okay? I don't want you out there wandering the streets on your own. Where have you been all this time?'

Roberto looked sheepishly down at his worn-out shoes, but the smile stayed fixed to his face. 'Sorry

Mamãe, I was just playing football at the pitch with Bruno. I was only going to stay for a few minutes, I promise, but then we–'

'No, no, no – how many times have I told you, son?' interrupted Mariana. 'You should be studying hard for your future, not wasting your life kicking a ball around with your friends!'

With a sad sigh and another 'Sorry!', Roberto followed his mum inside. He didn't like causing trouble, but it was so hard to say no to a fun game of football, especially when he could see the floodlights of the Estádio Rei Pelé in the distance. That was the home of the best team in Maceió, Clube de Regatas Brasil, or 'CRB' for short.

Roberto dreamed of playing there one day in front of thousands of fans. That was how he would get his family out of poverty – with his football skills, not his studies!

'How was your day, son?' José Roberto asked later that night when he eventually got home. He was tired and stiff after standing for hours at his cart, selling bottles of water on the streets outside the

CRB stadium.

Most of the time, Roberto was a quiet, shy boy, but not when it came to his favourite subject. Straight away, he started telling José about his football match. 'You should have seen it, Papai – the ball flew past the keeper before he had even moved! Bruno said it was my best goal yet!'

While his father listened intently, Mariana rolled her eyes. 'Football, football, football – it's all you two ever talk about! Let's change the conversation – how was school? What did you learn today?'

Roberto didn't have so much to say about school. 'I learned lots of things, Mamãe, and I did well in my Maths test too. The teacher said I got the top mark in the whole class.'

His mum looked much happier after hearing that news. 'Good boy!' she cheered. 'I knew you'd be a smart one. But you mustn't waste that brain! If you use it well, you'll get a great job when you grow up.'

Roberto would do his best to make his mum happy and vowed to continue studying hard at school. But he also secretly worked on his football skills whenever possible because he knew what he really wanted to do when he was older – and that was to play for CRB as their superstar striker.

CHAPTER 3

FALLING FOR FOOTBALL

As Roberto sat at home after school, trying to study, he heard a sound coming from above his head.

CLUNK! CLUNK! CLUNK!

How strange! Were there pigeons or rats moving around up on the roof? No, Roberto knew what that noise was – it was Bruno throwing stones from outside. And he knew what that noise meant too – it was time for football.

Hurray, at last! Roberto's face lit up with a flashing smile. He couldn't wait to get out on the pitch and play. But first, he had to find a way to escape. That wasn't easy when his mum was at home. She would never just let him leave through the front door to go and 'waste his life kicking a ball around with his friends'.

His only option was to jump over the back wall. And that wasn't easy either. The wall was very high with spikes on top, to keep thieves out, and also to keep Roberto in. To play football, however, he was happy to take the risk. In the early days, he had fallen so badly that he needed stitches in his knees. But even that hadn't stopped him and now he was an expert escape artist. With a quick scramble up and then a careful jump down, Roberto was free!

'Come on, let's go,' Bruno urged his friend. 'The others are waiting!'

By the time they arrived at the concrete football pitch, both boys were sweaty and out of breath. The game had already started without them, but now four versus four could become five-a-side. Much better!

'You're late – what took you so long? Right, Bruno, you're with Gabriel and João,' Dedeu, the group leader, called out once he had the ball in his hands. 'Roberto, you're with me!'

João's shoulders slumped and Gabriel groaned.

It wasn't that Bruno was a bad player; it was just that Roberto was the best and everyone knew it. Whichever team he played for usually won.

With another quick smile, Roberto ran onto the pitch, ready to enjoy every single minute. As soon as the match restarted, he was off, racing into tackles as if it was the last game he would ever play. He was like a dog chasing a bone and he didn't stop until the ball was won. Then, he switched to attack mode.

Uh-oh, danger alert! As hard as Bruno tried, he couldn't get the ball off his best friend. It seemed to be stuck to Roberto's right foot as he weaved his way through them all and towards the...

GOAL!

'Yes, 1–0!' Dedeu cheered with delight. That was one good thing about being the group leader; you got to put the best players on your team.

And what a player Roberto was! Away from the pitch, he was a shy, happy guy who hardly said a word. But as soon as there was a football match going on, he became an absolute beast. Suddenly, he was a totally different character – brave, confident, determined. The transformation still surprised Dedeu, even after all those years of playing together. If it weren't for Roberto's familiar smile, he would think it was a different person!

Before long, Roberto was on the ball again. This time, he spun cleverly past Gabriel and then knocked a perfect pass through to Dedeu with the outside of his foot. *2–0!*

'Thanks, Roberto!'

The score 2–0 became 3–0, then 3–1, then 3–2, then 4–2. Every time Bruno and his teammates thought they might get back in the game, Roberto stepped up with something special – an unstoppable shot, or a no-look nutmeg assist. Until…

DING! DONG! DING! DONG!

It was another noise that Roberto knew well – the ringing of the church bells nearby. And he knew what that noise meant too – five o'clock, the signal that it was time for him to get home quickly before his mum noticed that he was missing.

'Sorry, gotta go – see ya tomorrow!' Roberto called out, as he rushed away from his beloved football pitch.

'No, you can't go now!' Dedeu pleaded. 'We haven't won yet – we need you!'

But it was too late; by then, Roberto was already halfway home. And with another quick scramble up and then a careful jump down, he was over the wall and back in front of his schoolbooks just in time to see Mariana poke her head around the door.

'How are you getting on with your homework?' she asked.

'Fine, thanks, Mamãe,' Roberto replied, hoping she wouldn't notice his shiny, sweaty face.

'Good boy, keep going!'

Phew! Roberto had got away with it again, but there was no chance he could concentrate on his studies now. 'What a game!' he thought to himself, replaying the best moments in his head. And the next day, he would do it all again. Football was even more fun when it was forbidden.

CHAPTER 4

RIVALDO, RONALDO, RONALDINHO... ROBERTO!

As her son got older, Mariana gave up trying to stop him from playing football. Banning balls in the house hadn't worked, because Roberto just did keepy-uppies with oranges instead! Clearly her son was completely obsessed and, according to all his friends and teachers, he was also very talented.

'See, in a few years, our boy could be Brazil's next superstar striker!' José Roberto told her excitedly.

Really? How many famous footballers had come from the north of their country? Not many! In Maceió, they were hundreds of miles away from the major clubs, who were all based in the big cities like São Paulo and Rio de Janeiro.

But the more Mariana thought about it, the more she realised that it didn't matter how Roberto got himself out of the poverty of Trapiche da Barra, just as long as he managed to do it. If football was his path to freedom, rather than studying, then her son should play ball.

'Thanks, Mamãe!' Roberto said with a smile as he ran off for a kickaround with his friends. Hopefully, he wouldn't need to jump the wall anymore. And one day, when he became a famous footballer, he would pay his parents back by buying them a big house in a nicer neighbourhood.

That was Roberto's dream and he was determined to achieve it, especially after watching Brazil win the 2002 World Cup.

What a team they had! Lúcio, Cafu and Roberto Carlos in defence, Gilberto Silva in midfield, and then the '3 Rs' in attack:

Rivaldo, Barcelona's wizard with the legendary left foot,

Ronaldo, '*O Fenômeno*', the best striker in the world,

And finally, Roberto's favourite of them all,

Ronaldinho, the most entertaining player on the planet.

Even at the World Cup, football's most famous tournament, Ronaldinho still showed off his full range of skills:

Tricks and flicks against Turkey,

Cheeky nutmegs against China,

And a beautiful assist against Belgium with the outside of his right boot.

Unbelievable! Ronaldinho was a joy to watch and young Roberto loved every minute of it.

But easily the most exciting of all was his magical display against England. With seconds to go in the first half, Brazil were losing 1–0. But then, from just inside his own half, Ronaldinho raced forward, fooling Ashley Cole with a beautiful stepover. *Olé!* As the other England defenders surrounded him on the edge of the area, Ronaldinho slipped the ball across to Rivaldo, who curled it into the bottom corner. *1–1!*

'Yes, you hero!' Roberto screamed at the TV screen.

And early in the second half, it was Ronaldinho to the rescue again. He fired a long-range free kick over the England keeper's upstretched arm and into the top corner. *2–1!*

As the goal went in, Roberto and his friends watched with their mouths wide open in shock. Unbelievable! But was that meant to be a shot or a cross?

'It doesn't matter,' argued Ronaldinho's number-one fan. 'We're winning and the guy's a genius!'

Nothing could stop Roberto from loving his hero, not even a silly red card later in the game. That meant Ronaldinho missed the semi-final, but he was back for the main event – the final against Germany.

'Don't worry, he's going to win the World Cup for us!' Roberto told his friends confidently.

In the end, Ronaldinho didn't score or set up either of the goals, but he was everywhere for Brazil, creating chance after chance for the other two Rs.

'How did Ronaldo miss that?' Roberto groaned. 'Ronnie put that ball on a plate for him!'

It didn't matter, though, because at the final whistle, Brazil were the 2002 World Cup winners. And as Roberto made his way home through streets

filled with celebrating fans, he dared to dream.
What if one day, he could win the World Cup for
his country, just like the '3 Rs'? In that moment,
anything seemed possible, but Roberto knew that he
had a long way to go. He had to keep practising hard,
on his own at home and also on the football pitch
with his friends.

There wasn't much space in their five-a-side games
for Ronaldinho-esque skills, but Roberto didn't let
that stop him. He controlled the ball perfectly, spun
his way past Gabriel and then fooled Fabian with a
beautiful stepover that left him lying on the floor. *Olé!*

Now, all Roberto had to do was stay calm and
score. But just as he pulled his leg back, he spotted
Bruno rushing in to block the shot. No problem –
change of plan! With a drop of shoulder, he slipped
the ball across to Dedeu instead. *GOAL!*

The other players watched with their mouths wide
open in shock. Unbelievable! Anything that Ronaldinho
could do, Roberto could do too. But as much fun as it
was running rings around his friends, he knew that it
was time to test himself against tougher opponents.

CHAPTER 5

CRB'S NEXT SUPERSTAR?

'How are you feeling, son?' Mariana asked as they arrived together at the CRB youth team centre. It was a big day for her Roberto – his first football trial.

At first, he didn't reply; he just stared, with a mix of awe and excitement. The pitch was much bigger than the one he was used to, and the grass looked perfect. It would be like playing football on a lovely carpet, especially compared to the concrete court in Trapiche da Barra.

'Roberto?' His mum nudged him, but he wasn't listening to her; he was watching.

The first young players were running out onto the pitch to warm up, wearing the bright red CRB club kit and what looked like brand-new boots. As they joked around, they juggled the ball with ease, showing off skills that he had spent weeks learning. Wow, they were really good! Too good? No, he couldn't think like that. His trial hadn't even started yet.

Finally he responded to his mother's question. 'Yes, Mamãe – I feel ready!' he said, trying his best to sound confident.

But Mariana knew her son well. She could sense the nervousness behind his happy smile, so she tried to boost his self-belief. 'Good luck, darling. You're going to be great – CRB's next superstar!'

With a quick wave, Roberto walked off alone towards the dressing room. Not that he really needed to get changed; he was already wearing his only football shirt and shorts, which were now too small for him. They would have to do, though, until he got his own CRB club kit. How cool would he look then? And how jealous would Bruno and Dedeu be?

In the dressing room, in silence, Roberto sat down and put on his worn-out boots. His big toe was starting to poke out of the right boot, but he knew that his parents couldn't afford to buy him new ones. Besides, in football, it was talent that mattered, not expensive kit. He was here to prove that.

'Welcome!' Guilherme Farias, the CRB youth coach, greeted him warmly as he walked out onto the pitch. 'You must be Roberto?'

Instead of speaking, Roberto just nodded and smiled.

'Great, well, let's get started!'

Farias wasn't at all surprised by the new boy's shyness; he was used to that, especially coaching thirteen-year-old kids. More importantly, did this Roberto look like a talented footballer, CRB's next superstar? The boy was quite tall for his age, but a little on the thin side. That was okay, though; they could toughen him up. Farias's first impression was that the kid lacked confidence, but it was hard to tell until he saw him in action.

Once the training session started, Roberto switched to beast mode. He raced around the pitch, chasing defenders, dribbling past opponents, and creating chances for his teammates.

As Farias watched, a smile spread across his face.
This Roberto was good – really good! He could do it all
and he played with such bravery and determination.
There would be no need to toughen him up after all;
he was already much stronger than he looked.

With a clever turn, Roberto skipped away from his
marker again and ran forward at top speed. He could
hear a teammate to his left telling him to 'Pass!', but
this time, he wasn't in the mood for sharing. As the
last defender backed away, Roberto shifted the ball to
the right and *BANG!*

*Gooooooooooooooooooooaaaaaaaaaaaaaaaaalllllllllllll
llllllllllllll!!!!!!!!!!!!!!!!!!!!*

It was one of the sweetest strikes that Farias had
ever seen from a young footballer. Right, decision
made.

'Well done, kid!' The coach clapped.
'Congratulations, you're coming to play for us.'

Soon the paperwork was signed, and Roberto
was officially part of the CRB youth team. He even
had his very own club kit to prove it. It was a proud
moment for all the family.

'See, what did I tell you?' José Roberto said to his wife. 'Our son is going to be Brazil's next superstar striker!'

That was Roberto's hope too, but it turned out that the position of striker was a very popular one. CRB already had lots of them, including a great goal-scorer called Willian José. Never mind, Roberto was happy to play anywhere! Whatever the coach asked him to do for the team, he would do it with 110 per cent energy and effort.

'Yes, that's it – brilliant!' Farias shouted enthusiastically as Roberto won the ball back in midfield with an excellent slide tackle. The boy was the ideal student – eager to listen and lightning-quick to learn. With his skill and work-rate, the kid could play anywhere – in defence, midfield or attack.

During his first few years in the junior championships, Roberto mostly starred in a deep-lying midfield role. There, he could control the game with his touch, technique and vision, playing clever passes through to Willian. Together, they were the dream team, winning game after game for CRB.

Roberto loved every minute of it and the club looked after him well. They even helped pay for him to travel to tournaments when his parents couldn't afford it.

But just when Roberto seemed all set to become CRB's next superstar, he met a dentist who could see that he was destined for even greater things.

CHAPTER 6

A DENTIST WITH A DIFFERENCE

Away from his day job as a dentist, Marcellus Portella was also a massive football fan, and a passionate supporter of CRB. He even helped out his club whenever players had problems with their teeth.

Though Portella mostly focused his attention on the CRB first team, he was always interested in its future superstars too. One day, when he went along to watch the Under-16s in action, an exceptionally talented player caught his eye. But it wasn't Willian José, the team's star striker; no, it was their hard-working creative midfielder who was everywhere, doing everything – tackling, passing, dribbling and shooting.

'Who's that?' Portella asked Farias at half-time, pointing at the player.

'Roberto Firmino,' the coach replied.

'He's brilliant, isn't he?' the dentist declared, expecting a very enthusiastic response.

But instead, Farias just nodded and gave a slight shrug. What?! Portella was confused – were they talking about the same guy? Roberto was easily the best player on the pitch!

Over the next few months, Portella kept a close eye on CRB's underrated playmaker. Surely, he couldn't be the only one who saw Roberto's huge potential? But when he asked the other coaches, they weren't that impressed.

'Yes, he's good,' they argued, 'but he's not even our best young player.'

Portella refused to believe that, though. 'No, I think you're wrong. Mark my words – that kid will play for the national team one day!'

It was a bold prediction and the CRB coaches thought he was crazy. Roberto, a future Brazilian international? No way! Portella knew that it was pointless to keep arguing his case, so he decided that there was only one thing to do – speak directly to the player.

At first, Roberto hardly said a word to him. He was still very shy and, naturally, he was also a bit suspicious of this dentist who claimed he was going to help him to become a football superstar. But the more Portella talked about Roberto's talent and the world of football, the more he began to trust him.

'Honestly, you could be playing for one of the big clubs in the south,' the dentist told him, 'like Santos or São Paulo.'

'Really?'

'Of course, you're incredible! And then after that, anything is possible. Have you heard of Pepe?'

Roberto nodded. Everyone in Maceió had heard of Pepe; the defender was a local legend.

'Well, he started out at CRB just like you and now he's playing in the Champions League for Porto! There's no reason why you can't follow in his footsteps. Look, here's an idea – why don't we put together a video of your best performances? Then we can send it out to some clubs in the south and see what they think of you.'

Roberto smiled. What a great idea! Even if it didn't work out, it was still worth a try. Because if one of Brazil's top teams did notice him, that was definitely his best chance of becoming a football hero like Pepe.

As soon as Roberto's highlight reel was ready, Portella passed it on to an old friend, Luciano 'Bilú' Lopes. Bilú had played for CRB in the past, but now he played for Atlético Mineiro in the south.

'So, what do you think?' Portella asked Bilú once he had watched the video.

Fortunately, his friend was a lot more enthusiastic than the CRB coaches had been. 'He's good – very good! I really like his style. He's got lots of skill and he works hard too – that's a winning combination when it comes to football.'

'Great, so did you think any of the big clubs might take him on trial?'

'Maybe, let me see what I can do.'

Bilú set to work and a few weeks later announced that Roberto would travel south for two big trials:

first, at São Paulo, the Brazilian champions, and then at one of Bilú's old clubs, Figueirense. It was all arranged.

CHAPTER 7

A TALE OF TWO TRIALS

Roberto wasn't ready for the rush of São Paulo. Woah – Brazil's busiest city felt like total chaos, especially compared to beach life in Maceió. The flow of cars and people never stopped and neither did the noise.

VROOM! VROOM!

HONK! HONK!

BOOM! BOOM!

ARGH! ARGH!

It was overwhelming and Roberto was homesick. But his trial for the world-famous club, São Paulo, the current champions of Brazil and one of the most successful teams in all of South America, was a huge opportunity for him to shine. São Paulo was where many superstars had started out, including two of Roberto's heroes from the 2002 World Cup: Cafu and Kaká.

Could Roberto be next? That was the plan, but after spending two frustrating weeks on trial, São Paulo decided not to sign him.

'Ridiculous!' Portella responded angrily, before calming himself down. 'Hey kid, it's not your fault; they didn't even give you a proper chance to prove yourself. They'll regret it one day, when you're worth millions! Oh well, don't worry, things will be much better at Figueirense. I've got a good feeling about this one...'

Roberto really hoped that Portella was right. At São Paulo, no-one had talked to him and he had hardly touched the ball! It was a relief to leave the big city behind and move on to Florianópolis. Things were quieter there and there were lots of beautiful beaches. Here, Roberto felt more at home and able to focus on the trial ahead.

'This is it,' he told himself. 'My last chance to impress.'

Figueirense weren't a world-famous football club like São Paulo, but they had been playing in Brazil's top division, Série A, since 2002. That was the league where national heroes like Rivaldo, Ronaldo and Ronaldinho had all started their careers and Roberto really wanted to test himself there too. If he could just impress the Figueirense youth coaches and then fight his way through to the first team, he had a chance of becoming a Série A superstar. And after that, anything was possible – a league title trophy, an exciting move to Europe, or who knew, maybe even a World Cup win with Brazil!

Roberto couldn't get carried away, though. He had no idea how long his time on trial would last; it could be days, weeks, or even a whole month. But one thing was for sure: there wasn't a moment to waste. He had to make a big impact at Figueirense as soon as he arrived. Otherwise, he would be heading back north to tell his family that he had failed. He couldn't let that happen.

Hemerson Maria, the Figueirense Under-17s coach, called his young players together at the start of the training session.

'Everybody, this is…' he began but then he couldn't remember the new boy's name. Even though he had only just looked at the list, he had forgotten it already. Oh well, he would just have to take a guess. '…Alberto.'

The boy didn't correct him, so the coach continued. 'He'll be training with us this week, so please make him feel welcome. Right, let's go!'

Maria wasn't expecting much from 'Alberto', especially in his first session. Usually, triallists took a bit of time to settle in and get used to their new team. So, when the coach saw him pull off a spectacular overhead kick within ten minutes, he was shocked.

'Wow, did he really just do that?' Maria wondered to himself.

After that, 'Alberto' had his full attention. The kid had an excellent first touch and his technique was exceptional. Speed? Yes. Strength? Yes. Skill? Yes, yes, yes! The Figueirense youth players were finding it impossible to get the ball off him, even when they had him surrounded.

But best of all was the boy's attitude. All game long, 'Alberto' ran and ran, battling bravely for every ball. Then once he got the ball, he wasn't a selfish show-off like so many young triallists. No, he was a humble team player, who just really wanted to win. Maria loved the passionate way Roberto played the game, like his life depended on it.

'We should sign him up straight away,' one of the other coaches warned. 'Before one of the big clubs steals him.'

When 'Alberto' scored a second overhead kick, Maria's mind was made up. They had a very special talent on their hands and there was no way that they could let him leave.

Roberto's trial was over after only thirty minutes.

'Congratulations, kid,' Maria called out to him. 'You're in – welcome to Figueirense!'

With a big, beaming smile, Roberto ran back for the restart. He had done it; his parents would be so proud of him! He couldn't wait to start playing proper matches for his new team. This was it: the start of his journey to becoming a Série A superstar.

'So, how is Alberto settling in?' Maria asked one of his coaches for an update a few weeks later.

'Ah yes, I wanted to talk to you about him...'

Uh-oh, Maria didn't like the sound of that mysterious reply. 'Why, what's wrong? Is he not happy here?'

'No, he seems happy – well, he's always smiling anyway,' the coach replied. 'No, it's about his name. He's actually called Roberto, not Alberto.'

Maria couldn't believe it – he had been calling him the wrong name all that time. 'What, are you sure? Why didn't he say anything?!'

The coach shrugged and smiled. 'He's just very quiet and shy, that's all. Don't worry, the kid might not be much of a talker – but he's a mighty fine footballer!'

CHAPTER 8

A LONG WAY FROM HOME

On the pitch, Roberto got off to a flyer at Figueirense, especially once Maria moved him further forward, from defensive to attacking midfield. It was a simple switch, but suddenly Roberto seemed like a totally different, much more dangerous, player. Closer to goal, he could link up cleverly with the strikers and make the most of his creativity. Plus, he could still chase back to put pressure on the opposition midfield. Perfect!

Off the pitch, however, Roberto found life really hard. He was still only sixteen years old and he was living alone, a long way away from his family and friends. When would he ever get to see them again?

He missed them all so much.

'Mamãe, I want to go home!' Roberto cried into the phone. 'Can you come and get me?

'My boy, things will get better,' she told him tearfully. 'I know it's difficult, but don't give up on your dream!'

His mum was right; Roberto couldn't stop now. Not when he would hopefully soon have the chance to play professional football. That had always been his aim and he was determined to achieve it. So, although he thought about Maceió all the time, Roberto stayed at Figueirense, even when his team was given a week off.

'Why don't you go home for a few days?' Maria suggested. 'You deserve a break!'

By then, Roberto hadn't seen his family for seven long months, but he shook his head. 'No, I need to keep practising,' he replied. 'I don't want to lose time. I will only stop when I've succeeded in doing something good with my life.'

Maria was impressed. Not only were those the most words he had ever heard Roberto say in one go, they showed real mental strength. With that kind of dedication, the quiet kid was destined to go far in football, maybe even all the way to Europe.

By 2009, Roberto was attracting attention from lots of foreign clubs. The Dutch club PSV Eindhoven had sent their scouts to watch him play, and so had the English giants, Arsenal. They had already signed one promising player from the Figueirense youth team – the left-back, Pedro Botelho – so why not make it two?

Roberto tried not to get too excited. Scouts often showed an interest in a player at first, but their enthusiasm could fade away when they found someone better. Besides, was Roberto really ready to leave Brazil? He hadn't even played for the Figueirense first-team yet! And what about his dream of becoming a Série A superstar?

However, when the French champions Marseille invited Roberto to come for a trial at their club, Figueirense couldn't say no. As much as they wanted to keep their young star, this was a chance for them to make some much-needed money.

So, armed with a letter from Marseille, Roberto set off on his own for France. It was a big, scary adventure for the seventeen-year-old, and it was about to get even bigger and even scarier.

The journey was supposed to be simple: Brazil to Spain, and then Spain to France. However, when Roberto arrived at the airport in Madrid, he was immediately stopped by the local police. Where was the document that said he was allowed to enter Spain?

'What document?' Roberto wondered, beginning to panic. He had no idea what they were talking about, especially as he didn't speak any Spanish. He tried his best to explain that he was on his way to France for a football trial, but the police officers didn't believe him.

'Wait here,' they ordered.

For hours, Roberto sat there in a crowded room, not knowing what was going to happen to him. Would he have to pay a fine, or could he even be sent to jail? He was hungry, tired, and terrified.

'Help me, Mamãe!' Roberto called home in tears. 'I'm stuck in Spain!'

Eventually, the Figueirense director, Erasmo Damiani, managed to phone the airport in Madrid, but despite his best efforts, the police were still suspicious.

'I'm sorry, the kid doesn't have the right documents,' they kept repeating.

So, instead of letting Roberto travel on to France for his football trial, they sent him straight back to Brazil on the next available flight.

After that awful experience, it would have been understandable if Roberto had refused to travel ever again, but no, he was still determined to achieve his football dream. He knew other Brazilian players who had overcome similar setbacks to make it big in Europe. Like Pepe, the famous defender from Maceió, who was now starring for Real Madrid!

So, a month later, Roberto set off for France again, this time on a direct flight that didn't stop in Spain, and he made it all the way to Marseille. Here he spent a whole month training with the club's reserve team. Although he missed his home, he did at least have some fellow Brazilians around to keep him company. Besides, most days he was too busy making an impression on the football pitch to think much about his family and friends.

'Excellent play, Roberto!' The Marseille coaches clapped and cheered.

Before long, they were convinced that he would be the perfect signing – young, hard-working *and* high-quality. What more could you want from a footballer?

There was one problem, though: price. Figueirense wanted one million euros, which was a lot of money to pay for a seventeen-year-old, even one as skilful and promising as Roberto. In the end, despite all the coaches' arguments, Marseille decided it was too high a price to pay, and they let him leave.

'Oh well, never mind,' Roberto thought positively as he said goodbye to Europe and started his long journey home to Brazil. 'I tried my best and it wasn't to be this time. But once I've become a Série A superstar, I'll be back.'

CHAPTER 9

MOST PROMISING PLAYER

Before he could become a Série A superstar, however, Roberto would need to help lead Figueirense back up into Brazil's top division. His club had dropped down to Série B for the 2009 season, but they were looking to get promoted again as soon as possible. There were plenty of experienced players in the Figueirense squad, but surely they could use some fresh new faces to provide extra energy and excitement?

'I'm ready for the first team!' Roberto thought to himself, but rather than say this out loud, he tried to show it in every reserve and youth team match he played. He just hoped that the senior coaches were watching...

Eventually, Roberto's impressive performances did catch the eye of the Figueirense manager, Márcio Araújo. And after a few weeks of training with the first team, he was named as a substitute for Figueirense's home game against Ponte Preta.

'Thanks, Mister!' Roberto said with a massive smile on his face. He had only recently turned eighteen and this was the best birthday present ever.

Roberto couldn't wait to share the news with his family and friends. It was a shame that they wouldn't be there to see his Série B debut, but he knew that they would be cheering him on, all the way from Maceió. And hopefully, he would make them proud.

At half-time at the Estádio Orlando Scarpelli, it was 1–0 to Ponte Preta, so Araújo decided to make his Figueirense team more attacking. He took off a defender, Toninho, and replaced him with...

'Roberto!' the coach called out. 'Get ready, you're coming on.'

Wow, he was going to play a full forty-five minutes! With a big grin that showed off his new braces, Roberto quickly took off his tracksuit to

55

reveal the team's black-and-white kit underneath, with Number 16 on the back. Right, he was ready!

But as hard as he worked, it wasn't the dream debut that Roberto was hoping for. Despite a late Figueirense goal, it finished 2–1 to Ponte Preta.

'Hey, you did well today,' Araújo told a devastated Roberto as he walked off the pitch. 'Remember, this is just the start for you, kid. Next season – that's when you'll become a star.'

That confident prediction turned out to be correct. When their 2010 campaign kicked off against São Caetano, Roberto was there in Figueirense's starting front three, alongside Marcelo Nicácio and Willian. And it was Roberto who scored their winner, the only goal of the game!

As the left winger looked up to curl in a cross, Roberto made a clever run to sneak in at the back post. 'Yes!' He watched carefully as the cross flew towards him, but at the last second, a defender stretched out a leg to intercept it. So close! The ball flicked up high into the sky and as it dropped, Roberto got ready to win the battle. He outjumped the defender with ease and headed the ball up over the diving keeper and into the net. *1–0!*

Goooooooooooooooooooooaaaaaaaaaaaaaaaaaallllllllllll llllllllllllllll!!!!!!!!!!!!!!!!!!!!!!!

Making a heart symbol with his hands, Roberto raced over to celebrate in front of the fans. It was only the first game of the season and he was already off the mark.

Six days later, Roberto again scored the winner for Figueirense. Midway through the second half, he raced forward to put more pressure on the Portuguesa defence. The plan worked perfectly. Intercepting a loose pass, he dribbled just inside the penalty area and then calmly fired a shot past the keeper. *2–1!*

Goooooooooooooooooooooaaaaaaaaaaaaaaaaaallllllllllll llllllllllllllll!!!!!!!!!!!!!!!!!!!!!!!

This time, Roberto ran over to the touchline and performed a dance with one of his teammates. He was having so much fun in Série B! Two goals in two games – yes, it was all set to be a very successful year for Figueirense's most promising player.

Although Roberto didn't score in his next five matches, he still played a big part for his team. He defended doggedly from the front and created chances for the other Figueirense forwards. His game was about a lot more than just goals, but it was only a matter of time before his next one arrived...

In the first half against Vila Nova, Roberto burst forward at speed, skipping past the tackles of two midfielders. What next? There was no easy pass available, so he decided to shoot instead, from nearly forty yards out. *BANG!* The ball dipped and swerved through the air, before squirming under the confused keeper. *1–0!*

Goooooooooooooooooooaaaaaaaaaaaaaaaalllllllllllllllllllllllll!!!!!!!!!!!!!!!!!!!!

'What a strike!' his teammates cheered as they wrapped him in a big group hug.

Even at the age of eighteen, Roberto was already a key player for Figueirense as they pushed for promotion. With win after win, they moved higher and higher up the table – from ninth, to fifth, and then all the way to second place. As long as they finished in the top four, the club would be back in Série A next season.

'Come on, we can do this!' the manager, Márcio Goiano, urged his team on.

Goiano was strict with all of the Figueirense players, but especially with Roberto. During training, he was always pointing out his errors and showing him ways to improve. That was because he could see the youngster's potential and he wanted him to make the most of it.

'Better. Now you need to play like that on match day!'

'Yes, Mister.'

Again and again, it was Roberto who made the difference for Figueirense. With the scores tied at 0–0, he had the quality to win the game.

A clever flick header against Brasiliense. *1–0!*

A quick-reaction rebound against Bahia. *1–0!*

With only a few more points, Figueirense would be promoted. Away at Ipatinga, Roberto set up the first goal for Willian with a lovely through-ball. Nearly there now!

Figueirense finished the season in style against poor Paraná – but only once Roberto had arrived on the pitch. When he came on in the fifty-fifth minute, his team was losing 2–1. But within seconds, he equalised with a stunning long-range strike. *2–2!*

Goooooooooooooooooooaaaaaaaaaaaaaaaaallllllllllll llllllllllllll!!!!!!!!!!!!!!!!!!!!

'Come on!' Roberto cried out passionately as he threw one of his shirts into the crowd.

Ten minutes later, he helped complete the comeback with an assist for Willian. 3–2 – Figueirense were going up to Série A!!

At the final whistle, the players stayed on the pitch to celebrate their achievement with the supporters. What a season it had been for Figueirense! But amidst all the singing and dancing, there was one doubt on everyone's mind – would the club be able to keep hold of Roberto, who had just won Série B's Most Promising Player award?

CHAPTER 10

HEADING TO HOFFENHEIM

After his superb first senior season at Figueirense, Roberto was now on the radar of the top European clubs. Marseille and Arsenal were still showing interest, but it was Hoffenheim, an ambitious team from Germany, who made the first move to sign him.

Back in the early 1990s, TSG 1899 Hoffenheim were an amateur team playing in their country's eighth division, but by 2010, they had climbed all the way up to the Bundesliga. How had they made such a rapid rise? Big investment was important, of course, but Hoffenheim were also very smart in the transfer market. The club knew where to find the best bargains and they had talent scouts in all the

right places – from Sweden to Saudi Arabia, from
Belgium to Brazil.

In fact, for the 2009–10 season, Hoffenheim's
forward line featured three Brazilians: attacking
midfielder Carlos Eduardo, left winger Maicosuel and
striker Wellington. By the summer of 2010, however,
all three had gone; Carlos Eduardo was sold to Rubin
Kazan for £18 million, while the other two went
back to Brazil. Although Hoffenheim had brought
in high-quality replacements – Ryan Babel, Kevin
Volland and Gylfi Sigurdsson – the team still lacked
some of that South American flair.

So, the club's Sporting Director, Ernst Tanner, set
to work trying to find the next big thing in Brazilian
football. One of his scouts, Lutz Pfannenstiel,
recommended a promising player that he had found
on the computer game *Football Manager*. And when
Tanner asked Hoffenheim's South America experts
for suggestions, that same name kept coming up:

'Roberto Firmino'.

After watching videos of Figueirense's young
forward, Tanner could certainly see why. Wow, what

a talented player! It was time for him to take a trip to Brazil.

But at the Série B match that Tanner went to watch, Roberto hardly got to play. What a disaster! Hoffenheim's Sporting Director had travelled all that way for nothing. Tanner needed to see a lot more of Firmino before he could make a decision about signing him, and so decided to go along to a training session at Figueirense's stadium. When he arrived there, however, a guard told him, 'Sorry, you can't come in – no spectators allowed today.'

Tanner didn't give up, though. He tried every trick in the book – he begged, he pretended he was a tourist who just wanted to see the stadium, and he even offered a little bribe – until eventually, the guard let him in.

'Thank you, thank you!' he said gratefully. 'They won't know I'm here, I promise.'

Once he had Roberto in his sights, Tanner didn't take his eyes off him. He followed him around the pitch, studying his every movement. And in his head, he ticked off Hoffenheim's requirements one by one:

Speed? Yes, he's got plenty of pace, especially when he dribbles forward.

Skill? Oh yes, he's full of samba flair!

Touch? Yes, his close control is incredible.

Balance? Yes, he moves very well, both on and off the ball.

Heading? Excellent, he's got a great leap and lots of power.

Defending? Brilliant, he tries to win back every ball.

For a lot of clubs, it didn't matter how hard a forward worked in defence, but Hoffenheim were different. Their manager, Ralf Rangnick, expected each and every one of his players to press and fight for the ball, starting with the strikers. That was the team's style and it would suit Roberto perfectly.

Attitude? Amazing, he always wants to learn and improve.

Even when the Figueirense coach called him out in front of all his teammates and criticised him, Roberto didn't react angrily. No, he listened calmly and then tried to correct his mistake. That impressed

the Hoffenheim Sporting Director even more than
his skills.

'Most players I know would have stormed off the
pitch straight away!' he thought to himself with a
smile.

A positive mentality was so important in football,
especially for someone who was about to play in
a foreign country. Roberto would have to adapt to
a whole new life at Hoffenheim, a long way from
home. However, he seemed to have the strength of
character to succeed.

As Tanner left the training session, he knew what
he needed to do next – sign that young attacker as
soon as possible. And that's what he did, for a fee
of £3.6 million. It was quite a lot to pay for a little-
known nineteen-year-old, but the Sporting Director
was sure that he would be worth it.

'Right, are you ready?' Tanner asked.

Once the question was translated, Roberto smiled
and nodded. Of course, he was ready! This was the
life-changing opportunity he had been waiting for,
ever since his unsuccessful trial at Marseille. He was

on his way to Europe again, and this time, he would be there to stay.

'Welcome to Germany!' Tanner told him as they landed at the local airport. From there, they travelled straight to Hoffenheim's brand-new Rhein-Neckar-Arena. Woah, it was huge, and it looked so modern. Roberto would have to get used to playing in front of much bigger crowds!

Wearing his smartest shirt and jumper, he posed for photos holding the club's bright blue shirt, with '22 R. FIRMINO' on the back. As always, he had a smile on his face, but it wasn't as wide and beaming as usual because, although Roberto was excited about his new European adventure, he was also nervous. What if he hated life in Germany? What if he was a massive flop and the manager didn't rate him? What if he couldn't get into the Hoffenheim team?

It wouldn't be easy, but in spite of his fears, Roberto was determined to succeed.

CHAPTER 11

A WHOLE NEW WORLD

Roberto had arrived in south-west Germany in January 2011, just in time for the worst of the winter. Brrrr, it was absolutely freezing! He had seen snow a few times before at Figueirense, but that was nothing compared to the weather in Hoffenheim, where it snowed and snowed for days, piling up high on the pavements. Even wearing a hat, gloves and scarf at training, Roberto still couldn't stop shivering. It was as if the cold had crept all the way through to his bones.

'Is it like this every year?' he asked his new Ghanaian teammate, Isaac Vorsah, who just nodded back glumly before adding, 'You'll get used to it, eventually.'

The weather wasn't the only thing that Roberto would need to get used to in Germany. There was also the culture and, hardest of all, the language. The club organised lessons for him straight away, but unlike with football, Roberto wasn't a fast or willing learner.

'I still can't understand a word!' he complained to his teacher in Portuguese. 'How do you say, "Pass me the ball" in German?'

Roberto would also have to change his approach to his sporting performance. In Brazil, he had been praised for his speed and energy, but in the endurance tests at Hoffenheim, he came bottom of the group. Oh dear, he would have to do better if he wanted to become a Bundesliga star.

'Don't worry, we'll work on that,' the club's fitness coaches told him.

After weeks of hard running, Roberto was finally ready to make his Hoffenheim debut in late February. But in his first six games, his team only won once, and he didn't score a single goal.

'Why did we bother bringing on Firmino?' the fans moaned when Hoffenheim lost 3–2 to Freiburg in the local derby. 'What a waste of time and money!'

The criticism hurt Roberto, but he knew that he was tough enough, and talented enough, to bounce back. He was a '*guerreiro*', a warrior, who could overcome any challenge.

In the next match against Eintracht Frankfurt, Roberto came on as a sub with fifteen minutes to go and the score still at 0–0. The stage was set for him to become Hoffenheim's hero.

'This is my moment!' he told himself as he ran on to the pitch.

Minutes later, Ryan Babel dribbled down the right wing and took a long-range shot at goal. The ball flew straight towards the Frankfurt keeper, but it was too powerful for him to hold. He could only push it down into the penalty area and hope that his defenders would get there first.

But they didn't. Roberto reacted first and fired a shot into the bottom corner. *1–0!*

Goooooooooooooooooooaaaaaaaaaaaaaaaalllllllllllll llllllllllllll!!!!!!!!!!!!!!!!!!!!

At last! With a beaming smile on his face, Roberto

whipped off his shirt and whirled it around his head like a cowboy's lasso. Then, with a passionate yell, he threw it high into the air. It was such a rush to score his first Hoffenheim goal.

Roberto managed to grab two more goals in the last two games of the season, and so there were great expectations for him ahead of the 2011–12 campaign. Now that he was playing with confidence, could he go on and become one of Hoffenheim's first-choice forwards?

Roberto started the next season in style. Away at Mainz, he rushed in to steal the ball off the centre-back and ran all the way through to score. Then a week later, he helped Hoffenheim crush Werder Bremen at home.

For his first goal, Roberto showed off his broad range of skills: the flair to flick the ball over the first defender, the strength to battle and win the header, and finally, the vision and technique to lob the keeper with his left foot.

Goooooooooooooooooooooaaaaaaaaaaaaaaaallllllllllll llllllllllllllll!!!!!!!!!!!!!!!!!!!!!

Roberto celebrated by taking off his shirt and dancing his way back to the halfway line. He loved having fun on the football pitch.

'Firmino! Firmino!' the Hoffenheim fans chanted his name. After a frustrating start, they had now fallen in love with their entertaining Brazilian forward.

And late in the second half, Roberto scored again. This time, he used his speed to burst through the Werder Bremen backline and then calmly slotted the ball into the bottom corner.

Goooooooooooooooooooooaaaaaaaaaaaaaaaaalllllllllllll llllllllllllll!!!!!!!!!!!!!!!!!!!

In man-of-the-match performances like this, Roberto made everything look so easy. Surely, he was a superstar in the making?

Nevertheless, Roberto would only reach that highest level once he could shine consistently every week. In his next fifteen games, Roberto added just one goal and one assist. There were more flashes of brilliance, like his solo strike against Borussia Mönchengladbach, but overall, he was still a work in progress. Roberto would need to do better than seven goals in thirty-three games if he wanted to be a real Bundesliga star.

At the end of his third season, however, Roberto's numbers were still exactly the same. Yes, his game was about more than just scoring goals, but he had to become a more clinical striker. Otherwise, his team were in danger of dropping out of Germany's top division.

After finishing in sixteenth place, Hoffenheim had to fight for their survival in the 2013 Bundesliga playoffs. Would they win and stay up? Or would Kaiserslautern, the third-best team in the second division, defeat them and take their place?

Roberto and his teammates were really fired up for the first leg at home. Relegation would be a disaster; Hoffenheim were far too good to go down. They couldn't let that happen.

In the tenth minute, Kevin Volland won a free kick on the edge of the Kaiserslautern penalty area. Sejad Salihović curled it into the crowded six-yard box and there was Roberto, making a late run between two defenders, to flick the ball into the net. *1–0!*

Goooooooooooooooooooooaaaaaaaaaaaaaaaaalllllllllllll llllllllllllllll!!!!!!!!!!!!!!!!!!!!!

Roberto to the rescue! As he ran towards the corner flag, he jumped up and punched the air. Thanks to him, Hoffenheim had the lead; now, they had to hold on to it.

Twenty minutes later, Roberto dribbled in off the left wing, using his skills to skip past two tackles. After playing a simple pass, he moved slowly and stealthily into the space at the back post. So, when Andreas Beck slid the ball all the way across the six-yard box, Roberto was unmarked and in the perfect position to score. *2–0!*

Goooooooooooooooooooooaaaaaaaaaaaaaaaaalllllllllllll llllllllllllllll!!!!!!!!!!!!!!!!!!!!!

Blowing kisses to the crowd, Roberto led his teammates over to the touchline to celebrate with their substitutes and coaches. Staying in the Bundesliga was a big squad effort.

'Come on, keep going!' the manager, Markus Gisdol, urged his players on.

Of course 2–0 would be a good result for

Hoffenheim, but when Kaiserslautern scored early in the second half, Roberto knew that his team needed another goal. Receiving the ball on the halfway line, he turned beautifully and threaded it through to Fabian Johnson. When he lost the ball, Roberto won it back immediately. There was no stopping him; he was a man on a match-winning mission. With another perfectly weighted pass, he set up Sven Schipplock. *3–1!*

Schipplock was the scorer but Roberto was Hoffenheim's hero, with two goals and an assist. He had saved his best performance for their biggest, most important game of the season. Thanks to him, they were staying up in the Bundesliga, and an exciting new era was about to begin.

CHAPTER 12

THE BIG BUNDESLIGA
BREAKTHROUGH

At the start of the 2013–14 season, Roberto received
his greatest ever gift – the Hoffenheim Number 10
shirt. It was a famous football shirt all over the world,
but especially back home in Brazil. So many of the
nation's greatest players had worn that number:

Pelé,

Zico,

Rivellino,

Rivaldo,

And Roberto's ultimate childhood hero,

Ronaldinho.

'Thank you very much,' he said to Gisdol with a
big, beaming smile. 'I'll do my best to pay you back

with my performances, I promise.'

Giving Roberto the Number 10 shirt turned out to be a very smart move from the Hoffenheim manager. Roberto loved the responsibility of wearing it, and the freedom of his new attacking midfield role. On Matchday Two, he teamed up with his new strike partner, Anthony Modeste, to thrash Hamburg 5–1. Roberto scored the first and last goals, and in between, he grabbed a hat-trick of awesome assists.

He poked a through-ball into Kevin's path. *2–1!*

He delivered a dangerous cross to Anthony, who volleyed it in. *3–1!*

He dribbled into the Hamburg box, before cutting it back to Anthony. *4–1!*

'Wow, Firmino is on fire!' the German media exclaimed with excitement.

His Hoffenheim teammates, however, weren't surprised at all. They had seen Roberto's potential, his hard work, and his progress under Gisdol. Yes, in the past, he had played brilliantly one week and then poorly the next. But now everyone knew that he was ready to take his game to the next level, and no-one knew this more than his teammate, friend and fellow Brazilian, Christian Hening.

At thirty-four, 'Chris' was coming towards the end of his career at Hoffenheim and so he became a father figure for young Roberto. The two players often had dinner together and sat for hours, listening to samba music and talking about football. Chris had high hopes for Roberto, and he wasn't going to let him waste his tremendous talent.

'You're one of the best young players I've ever seen, but you've got to stay disciplined,' he often reminded Firmino. 'Every little detail makes a difference.'

If he wanted to become a Bundesliga superstar, then Roberto had to be the perfect professional. That meant always turning up for training on time, staying late for extra practice, eating a healthy diet – and getting the right amount of rest.

'You sleep too much because you're getting old!' Roberto liked to joke but he always listened to his friend's advice. It was already making a difference to his game. His body had never felt so good.

Roberto continued his fantastic form against Stuttgart, Schalke, Mainz and Hannover. The Bundesliga keepers tried their best to stop him, but he still found ways to score. Sometimes, Roberto dribbled the ball round them, sometimes he chipped it over them and sometimes he even slid it through their legs. But the result was always the same – GOAL! He was only one behind his previous Bundesliga best of seven already, and he still had twenty-four games to go.

It helped that Hoffenheim's new system suited Roberto really well. Whether he played out wide or through the middle as a second striker, Gisdol always encouraged him to do what he did best – defend aggressively from the front, putting their opponents under lots of pressure. Then, playing on the counter-attack, the team could make the most of Roberto's speed and skill. The plan worked perfectly, again and again.

And unlike previous seasons, Roberto didn't have any off-days or dips in form. Instead, he just got better and better. That Number 10 shirt was like Superman's cape! Away in Frankfurt, he set up Hoffenheim's first goal for Sven and then scored the second himself. At home against Stuttgart, Roberto provided two more assists for Sven and then fired a powerful penalty into the top corner. He was unstoppable!

What a good decision it had been for Hoffenheim to reject Lokomotiv Moscow's offer of twelve million euros for Roberto during the summer. He had developed so much since then and now he was worth double that money, if not more! Not that they wanted to sell him, though; what would they do without him?

By the time Hoffenheim took on Bayern Munich away at the Allianz Arena, Roberto had thirteen Bundesliga goals, plus eleven assists. The young Brazilian player was already enjoying a breakthrough season, but could he put in another big-game performance against the German champions?

'Come on, let's win this!' Roberto cheered with confidence. By now, he wasn't afraid of anyone.

At the end of a frenetic first half, the score was Bayern Munich 3, Hoffenheim 2. They were still in the game, but only just. The next goal would be crucial…

As soon as Kai Herdling won the ball in midfield, Roberto was off, sprinting between the Bayern centre-backs. He had timed his run brilliantly to beat the offside trap, but he needed the pass…

'Now!'

When it arrived, Roberto tried to cut inside onto his favoured right foot, but he found Dante blocking his path. Never mind, his left was pretty lethal too. *BANG!* The ball flew through the defender's legs, then past the keeper's outstretched arm, and into the bottom corner. *3–3!*

Goooooooooooooooooooooaaaaaaaaaaaaaaaaaalllllllllllll llllllllllllll!!!!!!!!!!!!!!!!!!!!

In a flash, Roberto's shirt was off, and he pumped his fists at the Hoffenheim fans. He felt like he could score against any team in the world. He was that good now.

'You hero!' Kevin cried out, throwing his arms around his teammate.

The year before, Hoffenheim had been fighting

relegation but now they were comfortably mid-table and even drawing with Bayern Munich. Although it was a team effort, of course, they had one player in particular to thank for that: Roberto Firmino. It had taken a few years to nail, but he now had the perfect blend of Brazilian flair and German grit.

With two more strikes against Borussia Dortmund and Eintracht Braunschweig, Roberto finished the Bundesliga season on sixteen goals. That was only four less than the league's top scorer, Robert Lewandowski. Not bad for someone who wasn't even a proper centre-forward! If you included the German Cup too, Roberto had an incredible twenty-two goals and sixteen assists from just thirty-seven matches.

There was more good news to come. Roberto was the deserving winner of the Bundesliga Breakthrough of the Season award. What a year it had been.

CHAPTER 13

STARRING FOR THE SELEÇÃO

News of Roberto's breakthrough Bundesliga season soon reached Brazil. Sadly, it came too late for him to make his country's squad for the 2014 World Cup, but after an embarrassing 7–1 semi-final defeat to Germany, the Brazil selectors decided it was time for big changes. They hired a new manager, Dunga, who called up lots of new internationals, including:

Alisson in goal,

Danilo and Miranda in defence,

Casemiro and Philippe Coutinho in midfield,

And... Roberto in attack!

On that special day when the brand-new Brazil squad was announced, Roberto was at a party to celebrate his dad's birthday. At first, when he answered the call from his friend, he thought it was a joke. But no, it was real! After a quick check online, Roberto let out a loud scream and then jumped around the room with joy. He had done it; his childhood dream was about to come true. The boy from Maceió was about to play for Brazil!

'This is my best birthday ever!' his proud dad declared.

Roberto started on the bench for their friendly against Turkey in November 2014, but midway through the second half, the *Seleção* were already winning 4–0. So Dunga decided to make a triple substitution. Off went Fernandinho, Oscar and Luiz Adriano, and on came Casemiro, Philippe and... Roberto!

Wow, what a moment! Proudly wearing his nation's Number 18 shirt, he raced on to the pitch to partner Neymar Jr in attack. Although he didn't manage to add a fifth goal, Roberto really enjoyed his debut for Brazil. At the final whistle, he walked off with a huge smile on his face. His international adventure was only just getting started.

Six days later, Roberto came on as a sub again, but this time in very different circumstances. Brazil were drawing 0–0 against Austria with thirty minutes to go, and so they needed a matchwinner.

'That's me!' Roberto thought determinedly as he stood waiting on the sidelines. It was the perfect chance for him to impress Dunga and secure his place in the squad.

Within seconds of Roberto entering the field, David Luiz made it 1–0 to Brazil, but they didn't hold on to their lead for long. It was 1–1, with only fifteen minutes left...

As Neymar dribbled forward, Roberto got into his favourite position – the gap between the opposition defence and midfield.

'Yes!' he called, but Neymar Jr passed it left, to Filipe Luís instead.

'Yes!' Roberto called again, still in that little pocket of space.

This time, he got what he wanted: the ball. As Roberto shifted the ball to his right, he thought about passing it to Neymar, who was racing forward into the penalty area. But no, for once, Roberto decided to be selfish and show Dunga what he could do. BANG! From outside the box, he fired an unstoppable strike into the top corner. *2–1!*

Goooooooooooooooooooaaaaaaaaaaaaaaaalllllllllllll llllllllllllll!!!!!!!!!!!!!!!!!!

Roberto threw himself into Neymar's arms, and then raised his right hand to the crowd. Yes, he was in the Seleção to stay! Hoffenheim's big game player had just become Brazil's big game player too.

Roberto's next two international strikes were also winning goals. First, he kept his cool in a one-on-one against Chile and then he cheekily nutmegged the keeper against Honduras. The timing was perfect. Brazil were about to compete in the 2015 Copa América, and Dunga was still deciding on his first XI for the tournament. In attack, Neymar and Willian were sure to start, but who was their best centre-forward?

'That's me!' Roberto thought determinedly. He didn't need to say it; he had already shown it in the best possible way – by scoring important goals out on the pitch.

For Brazil's first Copa América group game against Peru, however, Roberto found himself sitting on the bench. Dunga picked Diego Tardelli instead up front, but he didn't make that mistake twice. After Brazil escaped with a late 2–1 win, the manager returned Roberto to the starting line-up for the second game against Columbia. And even though Brazil lost 1–0, Dunga still stuck with him.

'You're our star striker now,' he told Roberto ahead of their last group game against Venezuela. It was a must-win match for Brazil, and they would have to do it without Neymar, who was suspended. Oh well, they had plenty of other big game players who were ready to shine...

Early in the first half, Thiago Silva volleyed the ball in from Robinho's corner-kick. *1– 0!*

And early in the second half, Roberto snuck in at the back post to convert Willian's cross. *2–0!*

Gooooooooooooooooooooooaaaaaaaaaaaaaaaaalllllllllllll llllllllllllllll!!!!!!!!!!!!!!!!!!!!!

With a confident wiggle of the finger, Roberto raced away to celebrate. 'Come on!' he yelled passionately, lifting Willian high into the air.

Brazil were through to the Copa América quarter-finals, but could they win another game without Neymar? That was the big question.

After the first fifteen minutes against Paraguay, the answer seemed to be 'Yes'. Brazil were passing the ball around beautifully, moving it left to right – Filipe to Robinho to Elias to Dani Alves... When Dani's cross came in, the ball was slightly behind Roberto, so with a subtle flick of his right boot, he left it for Robinho, who he knew was running in at the back post. *1–0!*

The Brazil players celebrated their brilliant team goal with a big group hug near the corner flag. Maybe they didn't always need Neymar after all!

The score was still 1–0 when Roberto was subbed off in the seventieth minute, but moments later, Paraguay equalised.

'Nooooo!' Roberto groaned. If only he was still out there, working hard to grab the winning goal, instead of sitting helplessly on Brazil's bench. But no, his game was over and soon, so was his first Copa América. When the quarter-final went to penalties, Roberto could hardly bear to watch.

'I should be out there taking one,' he thought to himself, 'and scoring!'

But instead, subs Douglas Costa and Éverton Ribeiro both missed from the spot, and it was all over for Brazil.

Although Roberto was disappointed, he didn't let it get him down for long. He was a positive person, and he could see the progress that he was making in international football. He had learned a lot from his first major tournament and hopefully, there would be plenty more future opportunities – starting with the 2018 World Cup.

CHAPTER 14

A PREMIER LEAGUE PLAYER

There was one other reason for Roberto's positive mood in the weeks after the 2015 Copa América – he was about to become a Premier League player!

The 2014–15 season had been another strong one in the Bundesliga for the Brazilian. Roberto hadn't scored as many goals as before, but that was okay because Hoffenheim had other players who could do that: Anthony, Sven, Kevin, Tarik Elyounoussi, Sebastian Rudy, and their new Hungarian striker, Ádám Szalai. What the team needed most from Roberto was his creativity and his clever movement to link the midfield and attack. He was Hoffenheim's most important playmaker.

Roberto set up both goals for Tarik and Adam against Schalke,

One for Kevin against Frankfurt,

Two for Sven and Sebastian against Hertha Berlin,

One more for Kevin against Mainz,

And one for Anthony against Hannover.

'Thanks Bobby, you're the best!' his Hoffenheim teammates told him again and again as they celebrated together.

Roberto was always happy to help others, but he loved scoring great goals of his own too. Away at Werder Bremen, he made a sudden sprint from wide on the left wing to meet Sebastian Rudy's long-range pass. He could see Raphael Wolf rushing out towards him, but Roberto controlled the ball and took it past the keeper with just one calm, clever touch. *Olé!*

And there was more magic to come. With an empty goal in front of him, Roberto decided to finish in style with a no-look shot. *Olé – 1–0!*

Goooooooooooooooooooooaaaaaaaaaaaaaaaaallllllllllll lllllllllllll!!!!!!!!!!!!!!!!!!!!

With ten goals, twelve assists and the sixth highest

number of tackles in the whole Bundesliga, Roberto had proved that he wasn't just a one-season wonder. He really was the ultimate all-round attacker. He could set them up and score; he could dribble and defend. It was no wonder that so many top teams were trying to sign him.

As the 2014–15 season came to an end, Roberto was one of Europe's most wanted men. Where would he go next? Would he stay in Germany and join the champions Bayern Munich, or take on a different challenge in a different country?

'All I can say is that he's moving to England,' his agent announced mysteriously.

So, which club would Roberto join? Arsenal, Chelsea, Manchester United and Manchester City were all interested, but it was Liverpool who eventually won the race to sign him.

The club had been following his progress for years, ever since he first arrived at Hoffenheim from Figueirense. The Liverpool scouts had watched, waited and reported back as Roberto got better and better, until eventually they knew that they had to act fast, before the other big clubs offered more money.

'Go get him,' the sporting director, Michael Edwards, told the club's chief executive, Ian Ayre. 'We need to do this quickly and quietly.'

Ayre was determined to get the deal done, and he didn't mess around. After agreeing a £29-million transfer fee with Hoffenheim, he flew to Germany and called Roberto's agent to arrange a meeting.

'Sorry, I'm in Chile with Roberto,' the agent replied from Brazil's Copa América base camp, where the team was preparing for their quarter-final against Paraguay. 'Can you come out here?'

No problem! Ayre always preferred to do business face to face, anyway. It was more personal that way and it was also easier to solve any problems. So, after jetting back from Germany, Liverpool's sporting director hopped straight on the next available flight to Chile.

Roberto, meanwhile, had a difficult decision to make. Was joining Liverpool the new challenge that he was looking for? It was a football club with a long and famous history, as well as a talented team in the present. They had come close to winning the Premier League title in 2014 and now they were aiming for the top again. But with Luis Suárez now at Barcelona and Raheem Sterling moving on to Manchester City, Liverpool were looking to build an exciting new attack...

'Come on, you'll love it!' his Brazil teammate, Philippe, tried his best to persuade him. 'The club is like one big family and the players are all really friendly. Trust me, the weather is pretty bad, but it's still better than all that snow in Hoffenheim!'

Roberto laughed. 'Okay, you've convinced me. Let's play together at Liverpool!'

Everything seemed set, until Ayre arrived at the Brazil base camp, and the guards told him, 'Sorry, no visitors are allowed in.'

Uh-oh, what was he going to do? How was he going to complete the deal and get Roberto to sign the contract? Eventually, Ayre managed to speak to Dunga, who agreed to let his player leave the hotel, but only for one hour. Luckily, that was all the time they needed.

'Welcome to Liverpool!' Ayre said afterwards, shaking Roberto's hand. Those two tiring flights – one to Germany, the other to Chile – had been worth it in the end.

Before he switched his focus back to Brazil's big Copa América clash, Roberto posed for his first photos wearing the red shirt. With two thumbs up, he gave his biggest grin for the cameras. He couldn't wait to get started at his new club.

Two weeks later, Roberto was on his way to England. 'Liverpool, here I come!' he posted for his Instagram followers with a picture of the club's famous 'You'll Never Walk Alone' gate. He had a good feeling about his latest football adventure.

After passing his medical, Roberto sorted out his new shirt number – 11 – and then took his first trip to Melwood, Liverpool's training ground. It was time to meet his new teammates and start preparing for his first season as a Premier League player.

CHAPTER 15

CLICKING WITH KLOPP

The Liverpool supporters had high hopes for their second most expensive signing ever.

'Coutinho and Firmino – that's double trouble for any defence!'

'Yeah, forget Sterling – this guy is going to be the next Suárez!'

In his first six Premier League appearances, however, Roberto didn't get a single goal or assist. Each time, he either came off the bench late in the second half or was subbed off after sixty minutes.

'Well played,' the Liverpool manager, Brendan Rodgers, kept telling him but Roberto couldn't help feeling frustrated. He knew that it was going to take time to adapt to the speed and physicality of English football, but he was also playing out of position. For some reason, Rodgers seemed to think that he was a right winger, or even a wing-back!

To make matters worse, Roberto then injured his back against Carlisle United in the League Cup.

'What a terrible start!' he thought to himself as he hobbled off the field in the first half.

But fortunately, everything changed for Roberto in early October. After a poor start to the season, Liverpool decided to replace Rodgers with the former Borussia Dortmund manager, Jürgen Klopp. For Roberto, it was excellent news. He had played against Klopp's team lots of times during his Bundesliga days and he knew the German's preferred style of football: forwards pressing from the front and playing quickly on the counter-attack. That suited him perfectly!

And Klopp was equally as excited about working with Roberto. He knew how clever and hard-working the Brazilian was and he had big plans for getting the best out of him at Liverpool.

'Don't worry, soon the fans will be saying,
"Firmino – what a fantastic signing!"'

As soon as Roberto recovered from his back injury,
Klopp moved him into the middle of the pitch to
play as the team's centre-forward. But the Liverpool
manager didn't want him to just stand up front as a
big, tall target man. No, he wanted Roberto to play
with freedom like he had at Hoffenheim, sometimes
dropping deep and sometimes drifting out wide, but
always making life really difficult for defenders.

'Yes, Boss!' he said with a big smile. He could
definitely do that.

Roberto's performances improved immediately,
especially in the big games. Liverpool were losing
1–0 to the champions Chelsea when he received a
pass from James Milner with his back to goal, just
inside the penalty area. He thought about trying to
turn quickly, but no, John Terry was right behind
him. So instead, he poked a clever pass across to
Philippe, who curled a spectacular shot into the net.
1–1 – the comeback was on!

Then a few weeks later, Roberto was on fire away

at Manchester City. Again, Liverpool's boys from Brazil linked up brilliantly.

Roberto raced onto Philippe's pass and tried to play it back for the one-two, but Eliaquim Mangala kicked the ball into his own net. *1–0!*

On another quick counter-attack, Roberto skipped past the City left-back and then slid a perfect, defence-splitting pass through to Philippe. *2–0!*

'What a ball!' Philippe screamed, pointing at Roberto as he slid across the grass in celebration. 'Now, you need to get your first Liverpool goal!'

It didn't take long to arrive. With a wonderful backheel, Emre Can played it through to Philippe in the penalty area. He could have taken the shot himself but instead, he squared it to Roberto for a simple tap-in. It wasn't the right time for his favourite no-look finish yet, though. He wanted to watch the ball cross the line. *3–0!*

Goooooooooooooooooooooaaaaaaaaaaaaaaaalllllllllllll llllllllllllll!!!!!!!!!!!!!!!!!!

'Congratulations, mate!' Philippe cheered the loudest as all the Liverpool players hugged their new scorer.

Now that he was off the mark at last, Roberto's smile beamed even more brightly. Hopefully, that would be the first of many goals at the club.

His next two goals took a while to arrive but they were definitely worth the wait. With a packed Anfield stadium roaring him on, Roberto scored twice against Arsenal. The first was a powerful strike and the second was even better. As the ball came to him just outside the box, there were four Arsenal defenders trying to close him down. Roberto had to act fast, and he did. With a quick tap and swivel, he curled a stunning shot into the top corner. *2–1!*

Goooooooooooooooooooooaaaaaaaaaaaaaaaallllllllllll lllllllllllllll!!!!!!!!!!!!!!!!!!!!

It was a beauty – one of the best goals Roberto had ever scored. As he ran over to celebrate in front of the Liverpool fans, he finally felt like a proper Premier League player now – even if the game finished as a 3–3 draw.

And the goals and assists kept coming:

Two calm finishes and a flick for Jordan Henderson

against Norwich,

A towering header and an unselfish pass to Adam Lallana against Sunderland,

A cross to 'Milly' and then a clinical strike against Manchester City.

After a terrible start, Roberto had really clicked with Klopp and successfully turned his first Liverpool season around. He even finished as their top scorer in the Premier League with ten goals.

However, Roberto offered his team a lot more than just goals. He was a forward with many talents; dogged in defence as well as amazing in attack. And his eleven assists were just as important as his finishes, especially in the Europa League semi-finals against Villarreal. After a 1–0 first leg defeat, Liverpool knew that they had work to do back at Anfield. It was time for Roberto to step up and be a big game player again.

He fired a dangerous cross into the six-yard box, which deflected in off a defender. *1– 1!*

He flicked the ball up over one opponent, chested it down and then volleyed a perfect pass through to

Daniel Sturridge. *2–1!*

He dribbled in off the left wing, using his skill and strength to beat the defender, before pulling the ball back into the middle. Daniel missed his kick, but Adam was there to score instead. *3–1!*

Hurray, Liverpool were through to the Europa League Final!

Sadly, The Reds lost it 3–1 against Sevilla, but Roberto stayed positive in defeat. Klopp was going to need time to build his brilliant new Liverpool team. The trophies would come eventually; Roberto was confident about that.

CHAPTER 16

FUN WITH PHILIPPE AND SADIO

During the summer of 2016, Klopp added a few more key pieces to his Liverpool puzzle.

Centre-back Joël Matip,

Midfielder Gini Wijnaldum,

And most exciting of all, his new forward, Sadio Mané.

Even in his very first training session, Roberto could see that Sadio was going to be an excellent signing. The Senegalese international was so speedy and skilful, with a ball at his feet, and even when he didn't have it, he worked really hard to win it back. If a defender took too long to play a pass, Sadio was there and ready to pounce. He was already used to playing a quick pressing style from his time at Southampton.

Roberto, Philippe and Sadio – yes, Liverpool's new attack looked absolutely lethal. With four Premier League games played, they already had two goals each. Together, they passed and moved all over the pitch, bringing out the best in each other.

Racing onto Milly's pass, Roberto cut inside, past the Leicester City centre-backs, and then sent Kasper Schmeichel the wrong way. *1–0!*

Sadio beat Schmeichel to Hendo's throughball and then squared it to Roberto, who calmly passed it into the empty net. *4–1!*

What a sensational start to the season! The goals kept coming and so did the wins, taking Liverpool higher and higher up the table. They were really entertaining to watch, and they played like a team, making football look so fun and easy. Poor Watford had no way to stop them.

Sadio flicked on Philippe's cross. *1–0!*

Roberto passed inside to Philippe who fired a shot into the bottom corner. *2–0!*

Emre rushed in at the back post to head home

Adam's long ball. *3–0!*

Adam set up Roberto for a simple tap-in. *4–0!*

Roberto outmuscled his marker and played the ball across to Sadio. *5–0!*

Gini reacted first to a rebound in the box. *6–1!*

As he watched his team from the sidelines, Klopp couldn't stop smiling. Not only had Liverpool just walloped Watford for six, but they were also now top of the table!

Sadly, they didn't stay there long. From 3–1 up, Liverpool somehow ending up losing 4–3 to Bournemouth. What? How? Where was their defence? Roberto trudged off the pitch in stunned silence. Clearly, they weren't Klopp's mean, winning machine, not yet.

By February, Liverpool had slipped all the way down to fifth, but they were still fighting to finish in the top four. Roberto was desperate to play in the Champions League for the first time. It was Europe's greatest club competition and one of the main reasons for his move to Germany all those years ago. He wanted to follow in the footsteps of his Brazilian heroes: Cafu, Roberto Carlos, Ronaldo and Ronaldinho.

'Come on, we can do this!' Roberto told his teammates. Even though he was still pretty shy, when he spoke, people listened.

In early March, Liverpool faced Arsenal at Anfield in a battle between fourth and fifth place. It was their biggest game of the season so far and losing just wasn't an option. They needed their front three back to their lethal best.

In the ninth minute, Philippe headed the ball back to Adam, who played it wide to Sadio on the right wing. After taking a quick first touch, Sadio fired a low cross into the box. It flew past Philippe in a flash, but there was Roberto, arriving at the back post. *1–0!*

Goooooooooooooooooooooaaaaaaaaaaaaaaaalllllllllllll lllllllllllllll!!!!!!!!!!!!!!!!!!!!

It was Roberto's tenth goal of the season, but what he really cared about was winning the game. As the players celebrated, he hugged Philippe and lifted him high into the air. 'Keep going, we've got this!'

When Klopp's Liverpool were at their best, playing

fast, flowing football, they were simply unstoppable. As half-time approached, they moved the ball quickly from left to right: Milly to Gini, and then to Roberto. Roberto was about to play another short pass across to Adam, but then he spotted Sadio a little further away, in lots of space, and if only he could just squeeze the ball between two defenders…

His pass was perfect and so was Sadio's finish. *2–0!*

What a magical team move! And this time, Liverpool didn't stop defending or lose their concentration. At the final whistle, Roberto punched the air with passion. 3–1. It was a huge result and a big step in the right direction: towards the top four.

For the next two months, Liverpool's front three were on fire. Roberto won a penalty to earn a point against Manchester City, and then set up Sadio for the first goal in their Merseyside derby win over Everton.

Hurray, Liverpool were up to fourth! Now, they just needed to stay there. But after a disappointing draw against Bournemouth, things didn't look good.

'No more slip-ups!' Klopp urged his players.

At half-time against Stoke, however, Liverpool were losing 1–0. They had to fight back, but how? Sadio was out injured until the end of the season. Luckily, Klopp had two gamechangers on the bench: Roberto and Philippe. The boys from Brazil changed the game straight away with their quick feet and clever movement. Philippe scored the equaliser with twenty minutes to go. Now, could Liverpool go on and win the game?

From deep inside his own half, Gini played a long, hopeful pass over the top for Roberto to chase. Despite a slight injury, he was determined to reach it first before the Stoke defenders. As the ball bounced down in front of him, he decided to go for goal. Why not? He was on the edge of the area now and he could see that the keeper was off his line. BANG! Roberto could tell that it was a sweet strike straight away. The ball cannoned off his boot, up over the keeper's upstretched arm, and then crashed down into the net. *2–1!*

Goooooooooooooooooooooaaaaaaaaaaaaaaaaalllllllllllll llllllllllllll!!!!!!!!!!!!!!!!!!!!!

Such an incredible and important strike deserved a special celebration. In a flash, Roberto's shirt was off and flying high into the sky. By the time it landed, Philippe had jumped on his back, yelling at the top of his voice:

'Yessssss, what a shot!'

Roberto was delighted with his match-winning goal, and eight days later, he did it again. With seconds to go in the first half against West Brom, Lucas Leiva flicked a free kick goalwards and there was Roberto, racing in at the back post ahead of his marker. *1–0!*

Roberto to the rescue! Liverpool looked safe in fourth spot now; they would be back in the Champions League next season. For Roberto, football wasn't just about how many goals you scored; it was about how many big game goals you scored – and for him, that meant a lot!'

Besides, there was shortly to be another celebration off the pitch: back in his hometown of Maceió, in June 2017, he got married to Larissa Pereira.

CHAPTER 17

FROM FAB FOUR TO FAB THREE

There was a lot of positivity at Liverpool ahead of the 2017–18 season, and not just because the team was back in the Champions League. The squad looked more settled now and much stronger too, especially with Klopp's two latest additions: left-back Andy Robertson and forward Mohamed 'Mo' Salah.

Some fans remembered Mo Salah from his days at Chelsea, but he was a completely different player now. In his last year at Roma, he had grabbed fifteen goals and thirteen assists, and Klopp was confident that he could become even better in Liverpool's fab front four.

Sadio on the left, Mo on the right, Roberto in the

middle and Philippe just behind – wow, that was a lot of speed and skill for one football team!

Roberto couldn't wait for the new season to get started. It would be his third year at Liverpool, and it was time to kick on and reach the next level. He had the Number 9 shirt now and he was hungry for more: more goals, more assists, more tackles and more trophies. He was still waiting for the first winner's medal of his professional football career.

'Yes, I've got a good feeling about this season!' Roberto told Philippe with a smile.

In the first match away at Watford, Liverpool's front three all scored: Sadio, then Roberto and then Mo. Excellent! But somehow, the game ended in a 3–3 draw.

'We can't keep conceding so many goals,' Roberto moaned to Gini as they walked back to the changing room together.

Two weeks later against Arsenal, Liverpool played with a much better balance, performing brilliantly at both ends of the pitch. In attack, it was Roberto who led the way. First, he headed home Joe Gomez's cross, and then he set up the second goal for Sadio. *2–0!*

'Keep your concentration!' Klopp urged his players at half-time.

And they did. In the fifty-seventh minute, the Liverpool defence cleared a corner-kick away towards the halfway line. They were preparing for another Arsenal attack, when out of nowhere, Mo raced in to beat Héctor Bellerín to the ball. After a sixty-yard sprint dribble, he slotted a shot into the bottom corner. *3–0!*

Eventually, Roberto and Sadio managed to catch up with Mo, and Liverpool's fab front three could celebrate happily together. They were already on fire and their fourth member, Philippe, was about to return from injury.

'The Premier League better watch out for us!' Roberto cheered in the big team hug.

When Liverpool were good, like against Arsenal, they were really good: *3–0, 4–1, 5–1, 4–0, 5–0…*

Roberto to Sadio to Mo – *GOAL!*

Mo to Philippe to Roberto – *GOAL!*

Mo to Roberto, then back to Mo – *GOAL!*

Sadio to Emre to Roberto and then through to

Sadio – *GOAL!*

But when Liverpool were bad, they were really bad: 0–5 against Manchester City, 1–4 against Tottenham, 0–0 against West Brom at Anfield...

'Argh, how did I miss that?' Roberto yelled into the air, as his shot rolled just wide of the post. Soon, Mo and Sadio were screaming the same thing. The result meant that Liverpool were already eighteen points behind the leaders Manchester City.

If they really wanted to challenge for the Premier League title, Liverpool would have to be more consistent in attack and a lot more solid at the back. So, during the January transfer window, Klopp made a bold decision about what was best for his team. He agreed to sell Philippe to Barcelona for £105 million, and with the money, he bought a top new defender: Virgil van Dijk from Southampton. Fellow ex-Southampton player Sadio was excited by the prospect of Virgil's arrival: 'I know we beat them 3–0 a few weeks ago, but trust me, he's brilliant!'

Roberto nodded in agreement. Although he was very sad to see his best friend Philippe leave, he knew that Virgil was a player that Liverpool really needed in order to reach the next level.

'Good luck and thanks for everything!' Roberto told Philippe an as they said their emotional goodbyes.

'You too, my friend – and see you for the next Brazil games!'

From now on, Liverpool's fab four would be a fab three. Could they keep the goals coming? Oh yes! At Anfield, they showed Manchester City how clinical they could be. City had been unbeaten all season, but early in the first half, Roberto won the ball in midfield and Alex Oxlade-Chamberlain dribbled through to score. *1–0 – GAME ON!*

Leroy Sané equalised just before half-time, but Liverpool were in a battling mood. Alex slipped a pass through for Roberto to run on to, and he used his strength to beat John Stones to the ball. Now, it was time to show off his skill. With a beautiful chip, Roberto lifted a shot over Ederson and in off the post. *2–1!*

Goooooooooooooooooooaaaaaaaaaaaaaaaalllllllllllll llllllllllllll!!!!!!!!!!!!!!!!!!!

What a finish! Throwing his shirt into the air, Roberto raced over to the Liverpool supporters, calling for them to make more noise. They didn't disappoint:

FIRMINO! FIRMINO! FIRMINO!

Liverpool's third and fourth goals were all about defending from the front. Their super-speedy attackers didn't give City a second on the ball. Roberto led the press, then Mo, who stole the ball off Nicolás Otamendi and set up Sadio. *3–1!*

Two minutes later, it was Sadio on the chase. Ederson raced out to clear the ball upfield, but his kick landed right at Mo's feet. He wasn't going to miss, not even from over forty yards out. *4–1!*

The Liverpool supporters were in dreamland. They held their scarves aloft with pride as the sound of a new song rang around Anfield:

We've got Salah, do do do do do do!
Mané Mané, do do do do do,
And Bobby Firmino,
But we sold Coutinho!

City did pull two late goals back, but Liverpool

held on for a huge 4–3 victory. They had just beaten the league leaders, and soon they would have Virgil at the back.

As soon as he came into the team, the Liverpool defence suddenly looked calm and settled. For the first time all season, they even started collecting clean sheets: *3–0, 2–0, 2–0, 5–0...*

'Much better, boys!' Klopp clapped and cheered.

Things still weren't perfect yet, but Liverpool were definitely making progress. If their fab front three of Roberto, Mo and Sadio could score another fifty-seven league goals between them, and they had a better defence behind them, there was no reason why The Reds couldn't challenge City for the Premier League title next season.

But before that, Liverpool had a Champions League final to focus on.

CHAPTER 18

CHAMPIONS LEAGUE HIGHS AND LOWS

Right from the start, Roberto's first Champions League campaign had been a cracker. It was like he was born to play in the biggest games, against the best teams in Europe. After scoring against his old club, Hoffenheim, in the qualifying round, the goals had continued to flow during the group stage:

Three simple tap-ins against Sevilla.

Two more against Maribor.

And a right-foot smash against Spartak Moscow.

'I love the Champions League!' Roberto cheered, throwing his arms out wide like a true Anfield hero.

Liverpool were through to the knockout rounds for the first time since 2009, and they were aiming to go all the way. With Virgil at the back and the fab three in attack, they believed that they could beat anyone, starting with Porto.

The Portuguese champions didn't stand a chance. Sadio scored the first goal, Mo scored the second, and Roberto looked set to score the third. The keeper saved his shot, however, and the rebound fell to Sadio. Oh well, it didn't matter who put the ball in the net, just as long as it went in. *3–0!*

'I'll take that as an assist!' Roberto called out as he raced over to celebrate with Sadio.

In the Premier League, Mo was miles ahead as Liverpool's top scorer, but in Europe, the goals were evenly spread out. Sadio was now on five, Mo was on six – and so was Roberto, although before the game with Porto was even over, he'd made it seven; Milly's cross from the left was so good that Roberto couldn't miss this time. *4–0!*

Goooooooooooooooooooooaaaaaaaaaaaaaaaaalllllllllllll lllllllllllllll!!!!!!!!!!!!!!!!!!!!

On his way to the corner flag, Roberto spun around and kung-fu kicked the air. Liverpool's

Brazilian warrior was having the time of his life.

'Quarter-finals, here we come!' he cried out joyfully.

Next up, Liverpool faced their English rivals, Manchester City. It wouldn't be easy, but Liverpool had beaten them before. Klopp kept his game plan the same:

'Press high up the pitch and hit them on the counter-attack!'

'Yes, Boss!'

In the eleventh minute, it looked like Roberto had wasted a glorious chance to give Liverpool the lead. Racing onto a pass from Mo, he turned past Otamendi, but he couldn't put enough power on his shot to beat the keeper.

'Ohhhhhhhhh!' the Anfield crowd groaned in disappointment.

But Roberto didn't give up. No, never! When Kyle Walker tried to clear the ball away, he rushed in to make the tackle. With a poke of his left foot, Roberto managed to push the ball across to Mo.

1–0 to Liverpool!

As Mo slid across the Anfield grass on his knees, Roberto was right behind him. Football was a team effort and together, they were beating Manchester City.

'Come on!' Roberto roared passionately at the fans.

Twenty mad minutes later, it was Liverpool 3 Manchester City 0, and it stayed that way until the final whistle, thanks to their firm new defence.

'What a performance,' Klopp congratulated his players, 'but remember, it's not over yet!'

It wasn't. In the second leg, City scored in the second minute. *3–1!* Was that the start of an incredible comeback?

No – Liverpool weren't going to let that happen. Once the first City storm was over, they pushed forward and punished them on the counter-attack. Sadio sprinted through and Mo was there to finish things off. *4–1!*

What a relief! Surely, that was game over? But Roberto kept battling until the final whistle blew. He ran over to close down Otamendi, who panicked and tried to pick out a teammate in the middle. But

Roberto read his mind and blocked the pass. *ZOOM!* He dribbled into the City penalty area and slid the ball into the bottom corner. *5–1!*

Now that really was game over! They were safely through to the Champions League semi-finals, where they faced Mo's old club, Roma.

In the first leg at Anfield, Liverpool scored five, but they could have scored fifteen. Early in the first half, Roberto set up Sadio twice, but he missed the target both times. Then Roma's keeper, Alisson, made a good save to stop a shot from Mo.

'Nooooo!' Roberto howled, looking up at the sky for answers. Was it going to be one of those wasteful nights for Liverpool?

Roberto was determined to keep creating chances for his teammates. Eventually, they would score…

In the thirty-sixth minute, Roberto slid the ball through to Mo and with a swing of his lovely left foot, he sent the ball curling into the top corner. *1–0!*

'Finally!' Roberto thought to himself.

And ten minutes later, they teamed up again. Roberto dribbled over the halfway line and then delivered the perfect pass to Mo, who scored with a delicate chip over the keeper. *2–0!*

Mo wasn't celebrating against his old club, but that didn't stop Roberto. 'Yes, yes, YES!' he yelled, jumping up on his teammate's back.

Roma tried to get themselves back in the game, but that only made life easier for Liverpool's fab front three. Mo set up more goals for Sadio and Roberto, and then Roberto headed home from Milly's corner. *5–0!*

What a night, what a season! Roberto had scored his eleventh Champions League goal and Liverpool were surely through to the Champions League Final.

Or were they? Roma scored two late goals at Anfield and then four more in the second leg out in Italy. That made seven goals in total but luckily, Liverpool had eight. Phew!

'Well done!' Klopp congratulated his players. 'But if we defend like that against Real Madrid, Ronaldo is going to destroy us!'

Yes, their opponents in the final would be the mighty Real Madrid, Champions of Europe for the last two years in a row.

Roberto wasn't scared, though. His Champions League final dream was about to come true and he was determined to enjoy it. He was a big game player, and this was the biggest game of all.

'It's a one-off match,' he told his teammates. 'Anything can happen and we're going to fight until the end. We've come this far together, so why not one more win?'

But sadly, Liverpool's big night in Kiev would end in heartbreaking defeat. As hard as the players fought, it felt like everything went against them.

First, Mo was forced to go off with a shoulder injury after thirty minutes. Next, early in the second half, Loris Karius went to roll the ball out to Dejan Lovren, but Karim Benzema stretched out his leg and deflected it into the net. *1–0!*

Sadio equalised a few minutes later, but then Gareth Bale came on and scored a breathtaking bicycle-kick. *2–1!*

'Woah, what just happened?' Roberto couldn't believe his eyes. As brilliant as the strike was, it was such bad luck for Liverpool.

Still, they kept going, searching for another goal. Sadio's shot hit the post and Roberto's cross struck Casemiro on the arm.

'Handball!' he cried out, but the referee shook his head.

It just wasn't Liverpool's night. With ten minutes to go, Bale hit a swerving shot and it slipped straight through Loris's gloves. *3–1 to Real Madrid!*

All around the pitch, Liverpool shoulders slumped – game over. Roberto knew that his team didn't deserve to lose like that, but that was football. It could be such a cruel game sometimes.

'Hey, we'll be back.' Klopp tried to comfort Roberto as he sat down on the grass in despair. He had been hoping for a happier ending to his best year as a professional footballer.

Never mind, all the Liverpool players could do was learn from their mistakes and move on. At least Roberto had one more football tournament left to look forward to that summer. Yes, he was off to Russia to play in his first World Cup for Brazil.

CHAPTER 19

BRAZIL'S SUPER SUB

Thank goodness 2018 was a World Cup year. Just hours after his heartbreak in Kiev, Roberto was taking his mind off things with Philippe and the rest of the Brazil national team.

'I just want to forget about that night,' Roberto told his friend, 'and focus on winning the World Cup instead!'

Brazil were always one of the favourites to win the tournament, but this time, hopes were even higher back home. Under their new manager, Tite, they were playing like a proper team again at last. Their results showed real progress: seven wins, one draw, one defeat and seven clean sheets.

It helped that the Brazil's starting line-up was strong and settled:

Goalkeeper: Alisson.

Defenders: Danilo, Miranda, Thiago Silva and Marcelo.

Midfielders: Casemiro, Paulinho and Philippe.

Forwards: Neymar, Gabriel Jesus and Willian.

And what about Roberto? Well, he was the super sub, the gamechanger.

In Brazil's pre-World Cup friendly against Croatia, he came off the bench to score their second goal with a lob over the keeper. And a week later against Austria, Roberto played a fantastic one-two with Philippe to set up Brazil's third.

'I love it when we play together!' Philippe called out, pointing and smiling.

'Me too!' replied Roberto.

But for the first seventy-nine minutes of Brazil's first World Cup game, against Switzerland, he had to sit on the bench, watching and waiting to make his debut in the tournament.

The Switzerland game started well for Brazil,

with a lovely goal from Philippe, but then their opponents equalised early in the second half. Brazil needed to find a winner from somewhere, but as the match ticked by, their manager Tite brought on one midfielder and then another.

'What about a striker who can score?' Roberto mumbled grumpily.

Finally, he got his chance. After some last warm-up stretches, Roberto high-fived Gabriel and ran onto the field, ready to be Brazil's super sub again.

His first opportunity arrived within seconds. When the Swiss centre-back sliced his clearance up in the air, Roberto chased after it. The angle was tight, and the ball was bouncing high, but he went for goal anyway. His shot flew over the keeper and over the crossbar too.

'Arghhh!' Roberto groaned, sliding across the grass on his knees. What a brilliant goal it would have been! Never mind, he still had ten minutes to make an impact...

In the dying seconds, Neymar curled one last free kick into the Switzerland box. The ball flew over the head of the first centre-back and dropped down towards Roberto. This was it; his best chance to become a World Cup hero for Brazil. Roberto jumped and pushed his head forward with as much power as possible, but the ball didn't land in the bottom corner as he had hoped. Instead, the keeper saved it and Fernandinho couldn't reach the rebound. It was game over for Brazil, and a disappointing draw.

Roberto walked slowly off the pitch, wondering what might have been. If only he had directed his header further away from the keeper. If only he had put more power on it…

'Hey, don't worry,' Philippe said, putting an arm around his friend's shoulder, 'we're just getting started!'

Brazil's struggles continued in their second match against Costa Rica. They had shot after shot, but the score stayed 0–0. This time, Tite decided to bring Roberto on a bit earlier, to add more energy to the attack, but it wasn't working. Neymar and Philippe were so desperate to score that they were trying to dribble around all the Costa Rica defenders and shoot from crazy distances.

'No, pass it!' Roberto screamed out in frustration.

The *Seleção* were moments away from a second draw, when Marcelo curled a high ball into the box. That wasn't usually Brazil's style, but now they had Roberto, who was unbeatable in the air. With a determined leap, he outjumped both of the defenders marking him, before heading the ball down to Gabriel. As Gabriel tried to turn and shoot, Philippe raced in to poke the ball through the keeper's legs. *1–0!*

'Come on!' Philippe roared with passion as he ran towards the corner flag with Roberto right behind him.

At last, Brazil were winning! All over the world, their fans went wild and so did their players on the pitch. The subs were so excited that they even knocked over their manager by mistake!

'Sorry, Mister, are you okay? We scored!!'

In the final minute, Neymar tapped in a second goal to secure the victory. Phew! It was a huge relief to have their first 2018 World Cup win.

'Okay, now we need to find our best form,' the captain, Thiago Silva, told the team.

Brazil were much better against Serbia – so good that Roberto didn't even get off the bench. The result, another 2–0 win, put them top of Group E, which meant a Round of 16 meeting with the Group F runners-up, Mexico.

Although Brazil were starting to find their confidence, they would have to be careful. Mexico were a dangerous team on the counter-attack, as they had shown by beating Germany 1–0. Both teams had chances in the first half, but it was Neymar who opened the scoring early in the second, after a lovely one-two with Willian.

'Yes!' Roberto celebrated with the other subs on the sidelines.

But now that Brazil were winning, would he be stuck on the bench? No, with five minutes to go, Roberto came on to replace Philippe. It was just enough time to try and grab a second goal…

As Neymar dribbled up the left wing, Roberto sprinted through the middle, making a run between the Mexico centre-backs. Neymar took the shot himself, but the keeper saved it with his legs. The

ball rolled agonisingly across the six-yard box for
Roberto to tap into an empty net. *2–0!*

*Goooooooooooooooooooaaaaaaaaaaaaaaaallllllllllll.
lllllllllllllll!!!!!!!!!!!!!!!!!!!*

Roberto had run so fast to reach the ball that he
ended up in the back of the net too! But not for long;
with a waggle of his finger, he raced over to Neymar
and lifted him high into the air. It was time to
celebrate – Brazil were through to the quarter-finals
and Roberto had scored his first World Cup goal!

'Firmino should be starting up front instead of
Jesus,' a lot of the fans argued afterwards. But no,
Roberto was back on the bench for the next game
against Belgium. Well, until half-time anyway. By
then, Brazil were already 2–0 down, so Tite sent
on his super sub.

The *Seleção* attacked again and again in the
second half, and eventually Renato Augusto scored.
2–1, with fifteen minutes to go!

'Come on, we can do this!' the Brazil supporters
cheered.

Roberto turned brilliantly in the box, but his shot

flew just over the bar. *ALMOST!*

Renato ran through, but he failed to hit the target. *NEARLY!*

Neymar cut it back to Philippe, but he sliced his shot completely. *UNLUCKY!*

Neymar's strike was curling into the top corner, but Thibaut Courtois tipped it over. *SO CLOSE!*

At the sound of the final whistle, Roberto looked down at his feet and let his shoulders slump. Despite his best efforts, Brazil's 2018 World Cup was over. It was a horrible feeling to be heading home so soon, but Roberto just hoped that he would get another World Cup opportunity. And next time, maybe he would get to be more than just Brazil's super sub.

CHAPTER 20

LIVERPOOL'S LINK-UP MAN

'Happy to be back,' Roberto posted on Instagram in late July 2018, along with a video of him hard at work during Liverpool's pre-season training. There he was with Sadio, stretching, running and of course, always smiling.

Roberto had lots to be happy about. The sun was shining (for once!), a new season was about to start, and two new Brazilians had just joined him at Anfield: Fabinho, an experienced defensive midfielder from Monaco. And Alisson, one of the best goalkeepers in the world.

Alisson, Brazil's Number 1, could do it all – stop shots, catch crosses, play great passes and come

flying out of his box to make crucial tackles. He was
the perfect signing for Liverpool and Roberto had
played a key role in persuading his friend.

'You can thank me later!' he joked with Sadio.

At last, it felt like the Liverpool dream team was
complete. At the back, Alisson and Virgil would
keep things calm and keep clean sheets; in midfield,
Hendo, Gini and Fabinho would battle box-to-box
all game long; and in attack, Roberto, Sadio and Mo
would do what they did best – score lots and lots of
goals. And if they failed? Well then, they had their
flying fullbacks, Trent Alexander-Arnold and Andy
Robertson, to deliver lots of dangerous crosses. Yes,
Liverpool were ready to really challenge Manchester
City for the Premier League title.

'Let's win that trophy!' Roberto cheered as they
started the 2018–19 season with a 4–0 thrashing
of West Ham.

Although he didn't score any of the goals, that
didn't bother him; his role in the team was much
more important than that. As Liverpool's link-up
man, he was involved in everything: connecting

midfield and attack. Roberto never stopped running. There was no-one else like him; he was half-defender and half-striker! His dribble from deep set up Sadio against West Ham, and his quick pass set up Mo against Brighton.

'Thanks Bobby, what would we do without you?' Mo shouted as they celebrated with a high-five.

Roberto was a real team player, but when Klopp needed him to get clinical, he could do that too. He scored the winner against Leicester and then against Tottenham too.

Five wins out of five! Liverpool were off to the perfect start, but so were their rivals, Manchester City. It was going to be a terrific title race, but who would finish as champions?

When the two teams met at Anfield in October, the game finished 0–0, leaving them tied on twenty points each.

'Well done, that'll do,' Klopp told his players. 'The main thing is we didn't lose!'

As Liverpool arrived at the Etihad in January, they were still unbeaten all season and seven points ahead of Manchester City. Plus, they had just thrashed Arsenal 5–1, thanks to Roberto's first hat-trick for the club.

The first was one of his favourite no-look finishes,

The second was a sensational solo dribble, weaving his way past two defenders,

And for the third, he sent the keeper the wrong way from the penalty spot.

HAT-TRICK HERO! At the final whistle, Roberto grabbed the matchball and walked around with it tucked under his shirt, clapping to the Anfield crowd.

Now, four days later, was Roberto ready to lead Liverpool to victory again? Oh yes, he couldn't wait for the big game to begin. With a win at Manchester City, his team would go ten points clear at the top! The first big chance fell to Sadio. He raced into the box and slid a shot past Ederson, but the ball bounced back off the post. So close! It wasn't over yet though. As John Stones tried to clear it away, he hit his own keeper on the back of the head and the ball bounced backwards towards the City goal...

'That's in – that's over the line!' Roberto screamed

at the referee. But the goal-line technology said no, and just before half-time, Sergio Agüero gave City the lead.

Uh oh, Liverpool had to fight back in the second half. So far, Roberto had been surprisingly quiet but suddenly he burst into life. First, he had a shot cleared off the line, and then a minute later, a second chance arrived. Andy volleyed the ball across the six-yard box and there was Roberto, diving in at the back post. *1–1!*

Goooooooooooooooooooooaaaaaaaaaaaaaaaaalllllllllllll lllllllllllllll!!!!!!!!!!!!!!!!!!!!!!

It was one of Roberto's easiest headers ever, but also one of his most important. Thanks to him, Liverpool were level in the biggest game of the Premier League season.

'Bobby, you hero!' Mo and Sadio screamed as they hugged their strike partner tightly.

Unfortunately for Liverpool, there were still thirty minutes left, and City were desperate to win. They attacked and attacked, until eventually Leroy Sané scored.

'Noooo!' Roberto's heart sank as he saw the ball land in the net.

Manchester City 2 Liverpool 1 – their lead at the top was now down to four points. And two months later, after four frustrating draws, they slipped below City for the first time all season.

'Come on, it's only one point.' Klopp tried to lift his players for the last nine matches. 'We can catch them!'

Liverpool went back to winning game after game… but City did the same. The two teams were still separated by that one single point. It was the tightest title race in years.

Throughout it all, Roberto stayed as positive as ever. 'It's not over yet – don't worry, we're going to win it!' he tried to convince his teammates. But as he got ready to beat Huddersfield Town, Roberto felt a sharp pain in his leg muscles. 'Arghh!' He winced, stopping straight away. He knew that it was bad news.

'Sorry, you're going to need to rest for at least a few weeks,' the team doctor told him.

The timing was terrible – they still had three

Premier League games to go!

With Roberto supporting them from the sidelines, Liverpool won their last three matches, but in the end, it wasn't enough. Despite all their hard work and all those wins, they still lost the Premier League title by that one point. It felt so unfair!

But as he walked out onto the Anfield pitch for the end-of-season celebration, Roberto was smiling as always. How could he not be, holding hands with his two beautiful young daughters, Valentina and Bella?

Oh well, Liverpool would be back to win the Premier League next year, and for now, he had something else to focus on: he had to get himself fit for another Champions League final.

CHAPTER 21

CHAMPIONS LEAGUE COMEBACKS

Roberto's aim was clear from the moment he ran on to the field in the opening game against PSG: to lead Liverpool back to the Champions League Final, and this time, to win it, no matter what.

First, his team were going to have to fight their way out of a very tough group, featuring Red Star Belgrade, Napoli and PSG.

When Roberto came on to replace Daniel, Liverpool were winning, but with ten minutes to go, Kylian Mbappé made it 2–2. Oh dear, a draw at Anfield was not the start they wanted. It was time for a moment of Brazilian magic...

As Roberto got the ball on the right side of the PSG

box, he could see three teammates in the middle, calling for the cross. But no, he had a different idea. Instead, he dribbled into the penalty area, twisting one way and then the other to make room for the shot. After fooling three defenders, he fired the ball into the bottom corner. *3–2!*

Goooooooooooooooooooooaaaaaaaaaaaaaaaaalllllllllllll llllllllllllll!!!!!!!!!!!!!!!!!!

Roberto to the rescue! As Gini jumped onto his back, he placed a hand over his left eye, the eye he had injured three days earlier against Tottenham. No, nothing was going to stop Roberto and his team from reaching another Champions League final.

Despite three defeats, Liverpool squeezed into second place in Group C with a nervy 1–0 win over Napoli. Against the odds, they were through to the Last 16, and a battle with Bayern Munich.

'Phew, that was close!' Sadio said, looking relieved.

Not Roberto, though, who looked as relaxed and happy as ever. 'Don't worry, we're going all the way this year!'

After drawing 0–0 at Anfield, Liverpool's chances

didn't look good, but away in Germany, Klopp's team yet again found a way to win. Despite feeling ill for days, Roberto was determined to play. He wasn't going to miss a big Champions League night; his team needed him! So, he ran and ran until he couldn't run any more. And by then, Liverpool had the victory, thanks to goals from Sadio and Virgil.

'Quarter-finals, here we come!' The whole team celebrated together. Only two more rounds to go...

By the time Liverpool played Porto, Roberto had recovered from his virus and he was back to his all-action best. In only the fifth minute, he collected Sadio's pass, swivelled quickly and laid off the ball for Naby Keïta to strike. *1–0!*

'Come ooooooooooonnnnnnn!' Liverpool's goalscorer and goal creator ran towards the corner flag together, laughing and smiling. And there was more good news to come.

Roberto started the move himself with a pass inside to Hendo. Then he raced towards the back post to get ready for Trent's cross. He knew what would happen next. It was a plan they had practised so many times and it worked perfectly. As the ball came in, Roberto was waiting on his own in the six-yard box. *2–0!*

Goooooooooooooooooooaaaaaaaaaaaaaaaaalllllllllllll llllllllllllllll!!!!!!!!!!!!!!!!!!!!

With their quick passing and clever movement, Liverpool made football look so easy. They were on their way to the Champions League semi-finals again, and could anyone stop them this year?

Messi and Barcelona tried their best. Away at the Nou Camp, Liverpool played pretty well, but their opponents were absolutely clinical. By the final whistle, Barcelona were 3–0 up and feeling pretty confident.

'It's not over yet,' Roberto told his teammates. 'No way!'

He had only played the last ten minutes due to injury, and even in that short time, he'd had a shot cleared off the line. The Barcelona defence looked dodgy; Liverpool could do this, even without their link-up man. But ahead of the second leg at Anfield, they also lost Mo to injury. Could Liverpool really pull off an incredible Champions League comeback against

Barcelona without two of their fab front three?

'Yes, we can!' the others bellowed with belief.

Roberto was there at Anfield to cheer them on, and so was Mo, wearing a T-shirt with a special message for the team: 'NEVER GIVE UP.'

The Liverpool players listened. Within seven minutes, the comeback had started. Sadio pounced on a mistake and passed it through to Hendo. His shot was saved, but Divock Origi was there in Roberto's role to grab the rebound. *3–1!*

'Yessssss!' Roberto celebrated with all the other Liverpool supporters in the stadium. It was horrible not being out there on the field, helping, but he trusted his teammates to get the job done.

At half-time, the score was still 3–1, but it wasn't time to lose hope yet. There were still forty-five minutes to go, and a football match could change in a flash...

Trent crossed to Gini, who fired the ball in. *3–2!*

Then two minutes later, Gini scored again with a header. *3–3!*

'YESSSSSSSSSSSSSSS!' Roberto roared, jumping out

of his seat. The atmosphere inside Anfield was now absolutely electric.

Like any football fan, he had watched the videos of Liverpool's 'Miracle of Istanbul', where they had come back from 3–0 down to beat AC Milan and win the 2005 Champions League. Well, now it was happening all over again – this was 'The Miracle of Anfield'!

They weren't through to the final yet, though. The match was heading for extra-time, but what if Liverpool could score one more? With fifteen minutes to go, Trent caught out Barcelona with a quick corner-kick. He crossed it to Divock, who banged the ball into the top corner. *4–3!*

The Liverpool comeback was complete! Roberto was desperate to race over and join in the celebrations, but instead he waited impatiently until the final whistle.

'Yes, yes, YEEEEEEEEEEESSSSSSS!' he yelled up into the night sky. He was so, so proud of his teammates. They had pulled off the impossible to send Liverpool through to their second Champions

League final in a row.

That amazing night at Anfield ended with all the coaches and players – including Roberto and Mo – standing arm in arm, right in front of the fans, to sing the club's most famous song together:

Walk on, walk on,

With hope in your heart,

And YOU'LL NEVER WALK ALONE!

It was a magical moment that Roberto would never, ever forget. He felt so lucky to play for such a fantastic football club.

Liverpool's heroes couldn't celebrate for long, though. Soon, they were switching their focus to the next big game. They had to finish what they had started, by winning the Champions League Final. Would Roberto be able to recover in time? Yes, as the Liverpool and Tottenham teams walked out onto the pitch in Madrid, he was back! There was no way he was going to miss a big game like that. With their fab front three together again, surely The Reds had to win the trophy this time.

Liverpool were 1–0 up before Roberto had even

touched the ball. Within seconds of kick-off, Hendo chipped a ball over the top for Sadio to chase. With his speed, Sadio got to it first and as he tried to cross it into the box, the ball struck Moussa Sissoko on the arm.

'Handball!' Roberto cried out, along with every Liverpool fan and all of his teammates.

The referee pointed to the spot straight away, and after a check with VAR, the penalty was confirmed. Up stepped Mo, who beat the keeper with ease. *1–0!*

Once the first wild rush of emotion was over, Roberto calmed down and concentrated on the game plan. Liverpool still had a long way to go – eighty-eight minutes, in fact. Now, they needed to defend well and not let Tottenham back into the game.

Roberto wasn't at his brilliant best after weeks out with an injury, but he never stopped running and fighting for his team. Early in the second half, Klopp decided that he had worked hard enough and brought on Divock to replace him.

'Good luck!' Roberto told his teammate, trying to hide his own disappointment. It was never nice to be taken off, especially in a big European final. But the team was the most important thing. That, and the trophy. Liverpool were now less than forty minutes away from Champions League glory.

Tottenham attacked and attacked, but they couldn't find a way past Alisson. Then, just when Liverpool were preparing themselves for a nervy last ten minutes, Divock scored to make it 2–0. Game over, final won!

Now the smile was back on Roberto's face. When the final whistle blew, he ran straight on to the pitch and celebrated by doing a forward roll. They had done it; Liverpool were the new Champions of Europe! There were tears of joy and happy hugs all over the pitch. A year on from that painful defeat to Real Madrid, they had bounced back to reach the final again, and this time, to win it.

'CAMPEONES!' Roberto posted on Instagram the next day, with a photo of him proudly wearing his winner's medal around his neck and lifting the Champions League. His first professional football trophy, at last.

CHAPTER 22

TROPHY NUMBER TWO!

For Roberto, the football never stopped. Just hours after taking the Champions League trophy on a bus tour through the streets of Liverpool, he was on his way to Brazil to prepare for the 2019 Copa América.

'I guess we can rest when we retire!' Roberto joked with Alisson on the private plane.

Together, Liverpool's two Brazilians had a big part to play for their country. Alisson would have to be at his best to stop South America's top strikers. And Roberto? Well, he was no longer the *Seleção's* super sub. He was now their star centre-forward, especially with Neymar out injured. And just in case that wasn't enough pressure, Brazil were also hosting

the tournament, so the whole country would be
watching and expecting them to win.

It was a good thing that Roberto was such a big
game player. Pressure, what pressure? He was a
Champions League winner now and he wanted
more! It was an honour to represent his country at
the Copa América, and he was going to do his very
best to make the Brazilian people proud. Two trophies
in one summer – why not? This was his year!

In their first game, Brazil had to be patient, but
they were too good for Bolivia in the end.

Philippe scored from the spot. *1–0!*

Roberto chipped a beautiful cross right onto
Philippe's head. *2–0!*

Éverton curled a shot into the top corner. *3–0!*

Brazil were off to a strong start, but four days
later, they failed to beat Venezuela. How? The home
fans were not happy at all. Despite having eleven
shots, three goals disallowed, and 70 per cent of the
possession, the match finished 0–0.

'We need a striker who can score!' some of their
supporters argued, but Tite refused to drop Roberto.

Instead, the manager picked Gabriel Jesus to play alongside him against Peru. And straight away, Brazil started scoring goals again.

Marquinhos flicked on a corner and Casemiro bundled the ball in. *1–0!*

Roberto closed down the Peru keeper as he went to kick the ball. It bounced back off the post and straight to Roberto for one of his favourite no-look finishes. *2–0!*

Goooooooooooooooooooaaaaaaaaaaaaaaaaallllllllllll llllllllllllll!!!!!!!!!!!!!!!!!!!

'Yes, Bobby!' Philippe cheered as he chased after his friend. He was so happy to see Roberto's hard work paying off.

All of a sudden, Brazil looked back to their samba best. Dani Alves played a beautiful one-two with Roberto before smashing the ball into the net. *4–0!*

At the final whistle, Brazil won 5–0. 'That's more like it!' Roberto cried as the whole squad celebrated together.

So, had Brazil found their form at the perfect time? Not exactly. In the quarter-finals, they faced their old rivals Paraguay, and the match went all the way to penalties.

Roberto's first thought was, 'Nooo, not again!' but he quickly pushed that out of his head. They had to stay positive and win the penalty shoot-out. This time, he was still on the pitch to help his team. Scoring goals was his responsibility.

'I'll take one,' Roberto told his manager.

Gustavo Gómez went first for Paraguay. His shot was heading for the bottom corner, but Alisson made a super save. *Advantage to Brazil!*

Willian, Marquinhos and Philippe all scored for the Seleção, and now it was Roberto's turn. After a short run-up, he struck his spot-kick high and hard towards the top left corner. However, the ball whistled wide of the post.

'Noooooo!' Roberto groaned with his head in his hands. What a massive mistake!

Fortunately for him, the next Paraguay player missed the target too, and Gabriel stepped up to send Brazil through to the semi-finals.

'Come onnnnnnn!' All was forgiven, but Roberto

still wanted to make up for his penalty miss. He was supposed to be Brazil's star striker. The Copa América semi-final would be the perfect match to prove it, against Messi's Argentina.

After an even first fifteen minutes, Brazil began to dominate the game. Dani Alves dribbled forward and passed it right to Roberto, who fired the ball into the middle, first time, without even taking a touch. The cross was so good that Gabriel couldn't miss. *1–0!*

'Thanks, Bobby – what a ball!' his strike partner shouted over the noise of the Brazil supporters.

Argentina soon fought back, hitting the crossbar and then the post. Uh-oh, were they about to equalise? No, instead Brazil hit them on the counter-attack, just like Liverpool. Gabriel sprinted all the way from his own half to the Argentina penalty area before setting up Roberto to score. *2–0!*

Gooooooooooooooooooooaaaaaaaaaaaaaaaalllllllllllll llllllllllllll!!!!!!!!!!!!!!!!!!!!

Roberto and Gabriel – what a dream team! Brazil's heroes hugged in front of their wildly cheering fans. They had beaten their bitter rivals, Argentina, to make it through to the Copa América final.

'And we're going to win that too!' Philippe declared confidently.

Brazil's last opponents would be Peru, the team they had thrashed 5–0 in the group stage. Surely, the trophy was almost theirs already? No, they couldn't think like that. Peru were a different team now. Since then, they had beaten both Uruguay and Chile on their way to the final. If they weren't careful, Brazil would be next.

As Roberto walked out for the final, in front of 70,000 fans, his usual smile was gone. A serious game deserved a serious game face. The Brazil players could relax and have fun once the game was won. Until then, they were fully focused on football.

In the fifteenth minute, Gabriel broke free and delivered a deep cross to Éverton. *1–0!*

'Yes!' Roberto cheered, throwing his arms up in the air. They were nearly there now.

Peru equalised from the penalty spot, but that didn't stop Brazil. They pushed forward and took the lead again. Gabriel scored the second goal and then

Richarlison added a third in the very last minute. Game over – Brazil were the new Copa América Champions! The stadium rocked with the sound of happy home fans. Their players had made them proud again.

Brasil! Brasil! Brasil!

Later that night, Roberto walked around the confetti-covered pitch with the huge silver cup in his hands and a beaming smile on his face. First, the Champions League and now this, his second trophy of the summer. What a year 2019 was turning out to be!

CHAPTER 23

CHAMPION OF ENGLAND, CHAMPION OF THE WORLD

After a few weeks with family and friends in Brazil, Roberto returned to England and got straight back to work. The 2019–20 season was going to be a very busy season for Liverpool, with a whopping seven pieces of silverware up for grabs: the FA Community Shield, the UEFA Super Cup and the FIFA Club World Cup, as well as the FA Cup, the EFL Cup, the Champions League and, most important of all, the Premier League.

'Let's win the lot!' Roberto told Sadio and Mo. He wanted more of that trophy-winning feeling.

Sadly, the first – the FA Community Shield – went to Manchester City after extra time and penalties.

Never mind, Liverpool still had six more trophies to go, starting with the UEFA Super Cup against the Europa League winners, Chelsea.

Roberto started on the bench in Istanbul, but it wasn't long before Klopp called on his main link-up man. Without him, the Liverpool attack was struggling, and the team was losing 1–0.

'We need you to help turn things around,' Klopp told Roberto at half-time.

Roberto the super sub made an instant impact. He raced between the Chelsea defenders to reach Fabinho's ball first, but could he beat the keeper too? There was no time or space for him to shoot, so instead Roberto flicked it to his right, where he knew that Sadio was rushing in. *1–1!*

'We missed you!' Sadio shouted as Liverpool's fab front three celebrated the goal together.

With Roberto back in the team, The Reds looked so much better, but they couldn't find a winning goal. They thought they had it in extra-time when Roberto escaped down the left and pulled the ball back for Sadio to score. 2–1! But a few minutes later,

Chelsea went up the other end and won a penalty. *2–2!*

After 120 minutes, the Super Cup Final finished with a shoot-out. Roberto had missed his last spot-kick for Brazil in the Copa América quarter-final, but he was brave enough to try again. In fact, he went first for Liverpool, calmly sending the Chelsea keeper the wrong way.

'Come on!' Roberto encouraged Liverpool's reserve keeper, Adrián, before jogging back to the halfway line.

And finally, after nine perfect penalties, Adrián was the hero, saving Tammy Abraham's shot with his legs. Hurray, Liverpool were the winners and Roberto had his third trophy of 2019!

Right, what next? Liverpool had made a strong start to the Premier League season, and after ten games, already looked unstoppable. With nine wins and one draw, they were now a mean, winning machine, leaving Manchester City trailing far behind.

Roberto was happy to let Mo and Sadio get more of the goals and the glory, but when his team needed him, he was always there to score the matchwinner himself:

A super strike against Southampton,

A powerful header against Chelsea,

A crucial tap-in against Crystal Palace.

And with a brilliant shot away at Burnley, Roberto also became a record breaker. He was the first Brazilian to reach fifty Premier League goals. What an achievement! He even did a special dance to celebrate.

'Nice one, Bobby!' Mo cheered as he gave him a great big hug.

Liverpool looked all set to become the new Champions of England, but before that, they travelled to Qatar to challenge for the 'Champions of the World' crown. As the Champions League winners, they had been invited to compete in the FIFA Club World Cup against other top teams from around the globe. To win their second trophy of the season, and Roberto's fourth of 2019, The Reds just had to beat the Mexican club, Monterrey, and then the Brazilian giants, Flamengo, in the final.

Two games didn't sound too tricky, but there
were a lot of tired legs in the Liverpool team. Was
it one tournament too much for them? No, because
fortunately, Roberto was on fire. After scoring just
one goal in his last eleven games, he grabbed two
in two:

A last-minute flick finish to beat Monterrey,

And then an extra-time strike to defeat Flamengo.

Liverpool were the new Champions of the World!

For Roberto, it was unbelievable, beyond his
wildest, childhood dreams – four top trophies in one
year! Life didn't get much better than that, so he
did his best to enjoy the moment with lots of hugs,
smiles and funny photos with Alisson.

'Don't bite that too hard,' the Liverpool keeper
warned as they posed with their winner's medals in
their mouths. 'You might ruin those perfect teeth!'

Five days later, Liverpool were in action again in
the Premier League against Leicester City. So, did
the players look tired after their travels? No way,
especially not Roberto. He carried on his fine form
with two more goals.

'Mate, you're scoring more than Mo right now!' Robbo shouted as he chased after Roberto.

The goals did slow down after that, but the key moments kept coming. Roberto was such an important player for Liverpool. He scored the winner away at Tottenham, then the winner away at Wolves, followed by a hat-trick of assists against Southampton.

'Thanks Bobby, you're the best!' cheered Mo, and all his teammates agreed.

With win after win, Liverpool got closer and closer to their first-ever Premier League title. Surely, it was only a matter of time now; they were twenty-two points clear at the top!

But in early March 2020, everything changed. The Premier League had to stop because of the spread of COVID-19. It was the right thing to do in such scary times, and Roberto sent his best wishes to all his fans around the world. But what if they couldn't carry on? What if the season was over? Noooo, that would be so cruel!

For three long months the Liverpool players stayed at home, training hard and hoping that they would get the chance to finish things off. For Roberto, it was a nice chance to spend time with his family and practise playing the piano and singing, but winning the Premier League was never far from his mind.

At last, in late June, the season restarted, but sadly no supporters were allowed into the stadiums. That meant Liverpool would have to win the league at an empty Anfield. There wouldn't be the same emotion and excitement, but at least the fans could watch at home on TV.

'Let's win it for them!' Klopp urged his players.

Liverpool really missed their fans in the Merseyside derby, but a draw still took them one point closer to the Premier League title. And after a 4–0 win against Crystal Palace, they were almost there. In fact, if Manchester City lost their next match against Chelsea, then Liverpool would be crowned champions.

'Come on, Chelsea!' the players and coaches cheered as they sat and watched the game together in a local hotel. After lots of tense twists and turns and bitten fingernails, it was all over. Chelsea had won the match against City, and Liverpool had won the Premier League title at last.

'CHAMPIONS' Roberto posted proudly on Instagram with a photo collage of all the Liverpool players. What a big team effort it had been. He couldn't wait to hold yet another trophy in his hands. He was now a Champion of England, Europe, South America and the World.

Not bad for a Mamãe's Boy from Maceió! From the poor concrete pitches of Trapiche da Barra, Roberto had risen all the way to the top, to play at football's highest level, just like he had always dreamed of doing. Yes, there had been difficult days at Figueirense and Hoffenheim, but he had never stopped believing and working hard to improve. It was that determination, combined with his skills, which made Roberto such a superstar for Liverpool and Brazil.

FIRMINO HONOURS

Liverpool
🏆 UEFA Champions League: 2018–19
🏆 UEFA Super Cup: 2019
🏆 FIFA Club World Cup: 2019
🏆 Premier League: 2019–20

Brazil
🏆 Copa América: 2019

Individual
🏆 Bundesliga Breakthrough of the Season:
   2013–14

🏆 UEFA Champions League Squad of the Season: 2017–18

🏆 Samba Gold award for best Brazilian footballer in Europe: 2018

FIRMINO

9   **THE FACTS**

NAME: Roberto Firmino Barbosa de Oliveira

DATE OF BIRTH: 02 October 1991

AGE: 29

PLACE OF BIRTH: Maceió

NATIONALITY: Brazil

BEST FRIENDS: Philippe Coutinho and Alisson

CURRENT CLUB: Liverpool

POSITION: CF

THE STATS

Height (cm):	**181**
Club appearances:	**455**
Club goals:	**139**
Club trophies:	**4**
International appearances:	**45**
International goals:	**15**
International trophies:	**1**
Ballon d'Ors:	**0**

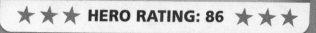

★ ★ ★ **HERO RATING: 86** ★ ★ ★

GREATEST MOMENTS

23 MAY 2013,
HOFFENHEIM 3–1 KAISERSLAUTERN

With Hoffenheim fighting for top-flight survival,
Roberto proved what a big game player he could be.
The Brazilian scored his team's first two goals himself
and then set up the third for Sven Schipplock.
Hoffenheim were safe and Roberto was about to
experience his big Bundesliga breakthrough

21 NOVEMBER 2015,
MANCHESTER CITY 1–4 LIVERPOOL

This was the day when Roberto proved that, with Jürgen Klopp's support, he was ready to become a Premier League star. After setting up Liverpool's first two goals with his hard work and passing, Roberto scored the third himself, his first in English football. This game was also to be the first of many big battles against Manchester City.

1 JUNE 2019,
LIVERPOOL 2–0 TOTTENHAM

This wasn't one of Roberto's best performances, but it did result in his first-ever trophy in professional football. After missing the 'Miracle of Anfield' against Barcelona due to injury, Roberto returned for Liverpool's second Champions League final in a row. This time, there were no injuries or goalkeeping gaffes; just a solid, if unspectacular, victory.

3 JULY 2019,
BRAZIL 2–0 ARGENTINA

With Neymar injured, Roberto took his chance to be
one of Brazil's star strikers at the 2019 Copa América.
He formed a perfect partnership with Gabriel Jesus,
especially in this semi-final win over Lionel Messi's
Argentina. Roberto set up the first goal for Gabriel and
in the second half, his partner returned the favour. With
a 3–1 win over Peru in the final, Brazil were crowned
South American Champions for the first time since 2007.

21 DECEMBER 2019,
LIVERPOOL 1–0 FLAMENGO

Roberto to the rescue! Against familiar opponents
from Brazil, he kept his cool to score an extra-time
goal and win the FIFA Club World Cup for Liverpool.
It was Roberto's fourth trophy of 2019 and soon, his
team would be Champions of England, as well as
Champions of the World.

PLAY LIKE YOUR HEROES

THE ROBERTO FIRMINO
NO-LOOK FINISH

STEP 1: If you want a goal, you'll have to work hard for it. Keep running all game long – putting pressure on defenders, but also racing forward on the attack.

STEP 2: When you get the ball with your back to goal, play a simple pass out wide to one of your flying full-backs, and then...

STEP 3: GO! Sprint as fast as you can to get into the six-yard box, either bursting between the opposition centre-backs, or sneaking in at the back post.

STEP 4: When the cross arrives, you'll have to act fast and use your skills. Dribble your way past any last defenders, and the keeper too.

STEP 5: Then once you've got an empty goal in front of you, great, it's time to finish! As you kick the ball across the line, look away over your shoulder, like you're too cool to care.

STEP 6: GOAL! Celebrate with a smile, a finger waggle and, if it's a really special occasion, a shirtless dance.

TEST YOUR KNOWLEDGE

QUESTIONS

1. What risky route did Roberto take to go out and play football with his friends?

2. When Marcellus Portella wasn't watching his beloved CRB, what job did he do?

3. Which two clubs in the south of Brazil took Roberto on trial?

4. What type of goal did Roberto score twice to convince one of those clubs to sign him?

5. Roberto was on his way to a trial at which French club when he was stopped by the Spanish police?

6. How much money did Hoffenheim pay to sign Roberto in December 2010?

7. What shirt number was Roberto given at the start of his breakthrough Bundesliga season?

8. Which two countries did Liverpool's chief executive visit to get the deal for Roberto done?

9. Roberto scored his only Liverpool hat-trick against which Premier League club?

10. Which two Brazilians joined Roberto at Anfield in 2018?

11. How many club trophies did Roberto win during the 2019–20 season?

Answers below. . . No cheating!

1. He jumped over the back wall 2. He was a dentist 3. São Paulo and Figueirense 4. Overhead kick 5. Marseille 6. £3.5 million 7. Number 10 8. Germany and then Chile 9. Arsenal 10. Alisson and Fabhinho 11. Three – the UEFA Super Cup, the FIFA Club World Cup and the Premier League

CAN'T GET ENOUGH OF
ULTIMATE FOOTBALL HEROES?

Check out heroesfootball.com
for quizzes, games, and competitions!

Plus join the Ultimate Football Heroes
Fan Club to score exclusive content
and be the first to hear about new
books and events.
heroesfootball.com/subscribe/